"Mind Over Meth ... eventual triumph o... Hedgcorth had descended into an abyss of drugs. This addiction consumed Debra and her family, causing years of heartache and hardship. There seemed to be no hope and no light at the end of the tunnel.

"All too often, this is where the story of the methamphetamine addict ends. By the Grace of God, Debra's story did not end that way. Debra recounts, in painstaking detail, the ways in which methamphetamine consumed her, causing harm to herself and to all of those around her. Just as detailed is her account of rising out of that life. Instead of accepting the life of an addict, Debra accepted Jesus Christ and He changed her life. She surrendered her life and soul, discovering a peace and joy that she had never known. Debra writes quite convincingly of the amazing change for the better her life has taken and the restoration of herself, her marriage and her whole family.

"Debra's story is tragic, shocking, inspiring and a testament to the power of Christ to transform a life. Her story also reveals a first-hand account of the devastation caused by methamphetamine addiction. It is my sincere hope that telling her story will discourage any and all who have considered "experimenting" with this dangerous drug to flee from it. Meth undermines communities, rips families apart and destroys life. It is also my hope that the telling of her story will encourage others to come forward and seek that same healing power that saved her life."

Governor Matt Blunt, Missouri

"*Mind Over Meth* is a vivid and harrowing description of the decent into drug addiction, and bondage. But it doesn't stop there. *Mind Over Meth* is also a testimony of mercy and deliverance by the power of Jesus Christ.

"Methamphetamine addiction is deceptive and seductive, making its users feel they can't live without it. In fact they are slowly dying, day-by-day…Debra Hedgcorth describes her turning point in which her little daughter standing on her tip-toes can see what Mommy is up to. The truth comes crashing in and The Truth delivers his precious child from slavery to that lie.

"Methamphetamine is a lie. It comes to kill steal and destroy. *Mind Over Meth* exposes the lie and offers life instead of death, hope in place of hopelessness. Addicts and their families will find encouragement to keep on fighting and keep on praying even in the face of the monster called meth."

Mary F. Holley MD
Founder and Director
Mothers Against Methamphetamine

mind

over

meth

Debra Hedgcorth

mind
over
meth

Tate Publishing & Enterprises

Published by Tate Publishing & Enterprises, LLC
127 E. Trade Center Terrace | Mustang, Oklahoma 73064 USA
1.888.361.9473 | www.tatepublishing.com

Tate Publishing is committed to excellence in the publishing industry. The company reflects the philosophy established by the founders, based on Psalm 68:11,
"The Lord gave the word and great was the company of those who published it."

Book design copyright © 2007 by Tate Publishing, LLC. All rights reserved.
Cover design by Brandon Wood
Interior design by Lindsay B. Behrens

Published in the United States of America

ISBN: 978-1-60247-863-3
1. Christian Living   2. Personal Life
3. Recovery   4. Self-Help
07.10.29

A true story of deliverance from addictions,
and the hope of abundant life.

Do not conform any longer to the pattern of this world,
but be transformed by the renewing of your mind. Then
you will be able to test and approve what God's will is...
His good, pleasing and perfect will.

Romans 12:2

dedication

I dedicate this book to my husband, Chris, and to our children, Tabatha and Samantha. When God laid on my heart the desire to write this book, I did not know the hours that it would take to see it through to completion. I am so thankful to my Savior that He would give me such a beautiful (and patient) family to share this life with. May God pour His blessings on them.

table of contents

foreword

Some have wondered if God, as revealed in the Bible, can reach to us in serious addictions and deliver us. When Paul, the apostle, wrote about this issue in I Corinthians chapter 6, he referred to people who practiced, and may well have been addicted to sexual sins, thievery, drunkenness, and so on. He celebrated the change in them by saying: *"...such were some of you. But you were washed, you were sanctified,* (set apart) *you were justified in the name of the Lord Jesus Christ and by the Spirit of our God."*

As a church family we have watched this miracle take place in the lives of Chris and Debbie Hedgcorth and their family. As you read of the tragic depths of addiction and despair, you may understand (perhaps for the first time as with me) the dark and hopeless pit that Meth addiction digs. This story will give you a better understanding and compassion for those in this horrible addiction.

Everything began to turn around as God's love and truth was shared through Christian neighbors and friends, bringing Debbie first to cry out her desperation to God. From that point the miracles begin to happen. Chris was next in seeking the

Lord for deliverance, and their lives begin to heal spiritually, in their marriage, physically and financially.

My prayer is that, as you read this, you will find fresh hope perhaps for yourself or others that with God, nothing is impossible and that when we believe and receive Jesus Christ we can find from Him everything we need *"pertaining to life* (physical) *and godliness* (spiritual)". [II Peter 1:3–11]

Pastor Tim Keene
Associate Pastor/Director of Counseling
James River Assembly of God

introduction

Mind over Meth. I don't know how else to say it. Originally, I felt that the contents of this book would be for people who are addicted to meth, people who have loved ones who are addicted, and finally, people who just want to understand, but I now know that it is for everyone. My prayer is that walls will be broken down, no matter what the issue is, and God will be glorified. As far as God is concerned…that would mean everyone.

The only way that we can get the right perspective about meth and the people who are trapped by its clutches, is to see things with a new set of eyes. Eyes that can see much deeper into the heart of man—passing all outer interpretations of what is really going on inside. I don't think that we consciously dismiss people who are struggling, yet that is the message that is quite often sent.

In the two years that I have been trying to put this story onto paper and into a publisher's hands, I have grieved for the families that are lost in a sea of regret, fear and a lifetime of pain. For my desire is to see them set free. That's the heart of our Lord Jesus. I am trusting Him to take this book to a people that will absorb the message, and join me in my journey to see

Him glorified. Through this story, I have had to say out loud many things that I would rather not have said. But, understand, it's not about me.

When I surrendered my life to the Lord, He showed me such compassion, and clothed me with such honor, and filled me with such strength, that I want the world to know of His mercy. He is and has always been waiting, and calling for each of us. His arms are never far away from those who put their trust in Him. Life becomes, not just possible, but beautiful.

This drug is sweeping across this nation, and blackening our continent. Our country, that has always been known as the "land of the free" is held in bondage by a horrific tool, used by our enemy, Satan. We do not have to be afraid, if we have the protection and strength of our Savior, Jesus Christ, to fight this battle. "As for me and my house, we will serve the Lord", in this fight…for the enemy has already been defeated. I just want to get the message out there to all who will hear, that they must simply come home.

life abundant

The thief (Satan) comes only to steal and kill and
destroy. I (Jesus) came that they may have *Life* and have
it abundantly.

John 10:10 ESV

The use of methamphetamines is, quite simply put, a mask used
to hide from real problems. I should know. I wore that mask and
that of other addictions for most of my adult life.

I was addicted to alcohol, pot, and pills for almost half my
life, and to the sale and use of meth for seven years. My husband
and I were both mired in that dark world. I felt no hope.

But then God performed a miracle and His grace brought
us out of that life, new and whole. This is the story of that deliverance; a redemption that you, too, can attain.

I'm thirty-five years old, the mother of two beautiful girls, the
wife of a wonderful man.

I love my life, but that was not always the case. For so long I hated my life, hated what I had become. But liberation from the prison of meth addiction changed all that.

I love to watch my family laugh with one another and share our favorite parts of each day as we sit around the dinner table. It feels like a fairy tale. It's better than anything I could have asked for.

My husband and I talk and laugh until we find ourselves even more in love than when we started the conversation. There are no hidden agendas, no lies, and no lack of respect that once ruled our relationship.

I love to watch my husband falling more and more in love with our children.

I no longer worry about what our children might see their daddy do because what they see is beautiful. They see him wake each morning to pray and read the Bible. He gathers the family together for a song to our Lord before we go to work and school and he prays a prayer of protection and blessing for us. We don't leave each other without this wonderful routine.

I love watching my daughters play together. We are trying to instill in them an understanding that they have been given an opportunity to be a blessing to each other.

Tabatha, who has Down Syndrome, is a master at being a servant, and loves to play for hours with her Barbies. Tabby takes every opportunity to clean and organize things and pamper those she loves. Samantha's strength is her giving heart. She would give away everything she owns if allowed. She's very bright and loves to play the teacher role as she works with Tabby.

If I'd been asked to describe anything about my family five years ago, I wouldn't have been able to see my blessings. But my wonderful God was blessing me even before I asked for His perfect forgiveness and chose to follow His perfect ways.

There was a time in my life when I mistreated my blessings. Like a spoiled child I was focused on myself, throwing a lifetime of temper tantrums. Day after day, year after year, I thought I had a reason for the anger I harbored, for every horrible thought that I indulged in, and for the addictions I allowed to control my life.

But in the last five years I have learned that it's not my job to change the past or to even hide from it. God says that we are to be transformed by the renewing of our minds, and the first part of that transformation is giving our life to Him. One hundred percent. Holding nothing back.

> God says that we are to be transformed by the renewing of our minds, and the first part of that transformation is giving our life to Him.

When I gave my life to Him, I began to see my past through His eyes. The view is a lot different from His perspective.

We each need to first realize that if we need a Holy God to rescue us, then there must be a reason to be rescued. The question is, rescued from what? The enemy, and his name is Satan.

Satan's goal is to destroy us, to paralyze us, and to rip away our hope. He doesn't care how he does it. In fact, he has many tools and many partners in his mission to drag us into Hell.

One tool Satan uses is our own bad choices. My bad choices led me into addiction to alcohol and drugs for most of my adult life, and deep into meth addiction. But God gave me hope, hope

I want to share with you. Because hope, true hope, lies in a loving God who is and always has been waiting with open arms to help us, and to fulfill our needs.

When God comes into your life it is by invitation only. He will never come without your invitation. But when we invite Him, we can stand completely free of guilt and shame. Yes, we *Stand!* No longer are we to crouch at the feet of Satan or be paralyzed by his rule of our lives. Because the enemy *has* been defeated. We now stand with the authority that Christ has given us to make him leave us. Praise God!

Meth is considered the most highly addictive drug known. Those held in its power feel there is no hope. But from God's perspective there *is* hope. I'm a living example and it's not just for me and my husband. It's there for everyone.

This is my story. A story that started in a home plagued by the addictions of my parents and continued in a life filled with the darkness of my own multiple addictions. But it is also a story of deliverance, of forgiveness, of salvation.

Please walk with me as I tell you about the transformation that is only attainable through Christ.

through my "child eyes"

When I was a child, I spoke as a child, I thought like a child, I reasoned as a child. When I became a man, I gave up childish ways.

1 Corinthians 13:11 ESV

I give you my background, my childhood, first because it sets the stage for what came later. My parents made choices that were not always the best for themselves, and not for us children. This background was no excuse for the choices I made, but is the basis for much of it.

My purpose for this book is not to shame my family in any way, but to allow moms and dads, especially those addicted to drugs and alcohol, to understand some issues that face our children. Issues of drug addiction and issues of faith. To that purpose I will relate what I remember from my point of view as a scared little girl, with my "child eyes", and even as a grown woman…until I found the Lord Jesus and He gave me His eyes to see.

When I was a small child, my family moved a lot; from county to county, state to state, and often in the middle of the night or so quickly that I had to leave a lot behind. It wasn't until I was in grade school that I understood that the reason we moved so much was because we owed bills, everywhere, and that people were quite often looking for my father.

> When I was a small child, my family moved a lot; from county to county, state to state, and often in the middle of the night or so quickly that I had to leave a lot behind.

I'll take you back as early as I can remember, about age five. My memory was that things were good in our family then. We lived in a house with a big back yard and I went to school half day. My mother kept a clean house and fed us hot meals. We read books and went on walks.

When my father was home, I entertained by standing on milk crates or other makeshift stages and singing songs like, "Whatcha Gonna Do With a Dog Like That" or "Beautiful Beautiful Brown Eyes". These songs described a home plagued by alcoholism. He praised me and promised that one day I would sing in the bar with him. That was my dream.

But that "dream" would not become reality, nor would others.

We moved many times and literally endured many bad situations that we will get to in the next chapter.

I loved my dad, but our relationship was terribly unhealthy and twisted. Like any other little child, I desperately wanted someone strong and comfortable and ready for any problem I had. But he was an alcoholic, drunk more than sober most of his life. As a child I thought that, like my mother, I would probably marry someone who drank a lot; but, of course, he would be able to control himself and be a successful man who took care of me. We spin our dreams at all ages.

We didn't have a phone. It was years before we finally had running water. There was a well to draw water from for washing dishes and for taking baths. In the summer, we filled an old cream can and let the sun heat it, then we'd stand out in our yard and pour water over ourselves, and called this our "shower". Since we were at the end of a long road, we could hear a car coming then run and hide while trying to get the suds out of our hair. We'd had running water before this move, so I knew how it felt to take a bath or a shower with running water which made me hate this situation even more.

There was always the promise—we'll get running water… any day. My dad was a drug addict and alcoholic and any money that came in was used to support his habit. For years we took care of our landlord's cattle and property to cover the rent.

Since there was no running water in the house, we used an outhouse for years. I thought it was gross—*I can't believe we're doing this!* But my mom tried to make it all seem like an adventure. She wasn't aware herself that she was slowly slipping into a depressive state, but this is the point where she started having difficulty keeping up with the housekeeping, and slept more during the day hours.

I want to explain again that my anger toward my mother as a child and young adult is what a lot of kids go through in situations where one parent or both are trapped in a life controlling problem. It's hard for a child to understand much more than their young minds can accept, and is the basis for many turning to life controlling problems themselves. I am blown away by the statistics which back up the fact that children of addicts/alcoholics tend to follow the same pattern in their lives. It doesn't make sense. But, children's minds are like little computers, always drinking up the information that is fed to them, creating a kind of basis for which they build their concepts. My mind was being fed so many different facts of what right and wrong were, I didn't know how to distinguish the two at times.

So here we are, in the middle of nowhere, no running water and a family of six. My mother would scrub clothes in the bathtub, sloshing them around until they were clean. She'd hold one end and one of us would hold the other to wring them out. She hung them out on the line in the summer months. In the winter, we hung them out to freeze dry then we brought them inside and hung them around a big barrel stove to finish drying. The stove was made from a fifty-five gallon steel barrel with a door placed at one end, and a pipe extending from the top for exhaust.

That stove was our heat for the winter months and when we didn't have gas for the kitchen stove, it was where we heated water to take baths, wash dishes, or for whatever else we needed.

We only had one bedroom in this house. The living room was pretty big so dad put up a partition and made a second bedroom that held two beds. My little brother slept in one and my sister and I slept in a double bed. Off the living room was a storage room just big enough for a twin bed, leaving maybe six to eight inches of room on one side. My older brother, Terry, slept there. When he left home, Jack inherited the room and he thought—*Oh! I've got my own room!* A storage closet.

So that was home. We thought we'd live there for only a couple of years, but my dad's alcoholism grew decidedly worse. Then he had colon surgery. The doctor said that dad's colon was full of, as he described it, "blow outs" from years of pills and drinking. He would have a couple of colon surgeries in seven years but the first colostomy, with the bag outside his body, hit his pride pretty hard. His anger grew worse than ever, and his addictions skyrocketed.

My father had a terrible temper, especially when he was drinking. He took his anger out on Terry, kicking him in the side again and again, telling him to get out of the way, that he was nothing but a lazy bum, not worth anything at all. When Jack got older, he would jump on dad's back to stop this from happening. My dad would throw him against the wall. Mom would jump in and he would turn his anger on her.

> My father had a terrible temper, especially when he was drinking.

Dad never hit me, but he wasn't the daddy he should have been to me either. He would kiss me, put his tongue in my mouth and touch my body…not often, but even the few times I remember made me hate to be alive.

In him, I saw a mad man, a man who in my opinion should have never had children because all he did was abuse them, as he had been abused himself as a child. I longed for a father who cared so much about his family that he would sacrifice anything to make sure we were cared for. I felt that if I could make enough good things happen, he would be happy with us, with his life. I eventually turned my fear and sadness into anger and started to blame my mother.

Now, through my Savior's eyes, I understand there was a deeper story.

Embarrassed by the way we lived, I allowed only a couple of friends I trusted to come over. Mom had really slipped into a state of not being able to cope and the house was always dirty. Both my parents were chain smokers and they left ash trays full and running over, ashes everywhere. The one or two times I did ask someone to come home with me, mom cleaned all week.

All day at school I worried and fretted and prepared a lie in case mom wouldn't have things clean. I would spin the lies from big to bigger in my head just in case I needed to use them. The worry that my father would come home drunk—well, I just hoped against hope that he wouldn't.

Mom always made sure we were fed good, hot meals. My mom can cook! At night she tucked each one of us into bed, then would sit at the kitchen table reading romance books, trying not to do anything to make my dad angry.

Some days she would sit at the kitchen table and fill tablet after tablet with mathematical problems, starting with one huge number across the top of the paper then start subtracting, adding, and dividing. If she wasn't reading or playing with numbers, she would draw pictures of her dream home. That was her fantasy world. Maybe when she was in that world she didn't have to think about what might happen next with my father.

When my dad worked for a construction company, he was gone sometimes for a week or two at a time. When she heard that my dad was coming home, she would whip through the house so quickly and have everything in order for his arrival. I wondered why she wouldn't do that daily; really I was looking for another thing to hold against her—I was angry at her for not keeping the house like other moms I knew.

My dad was the polar opposite of my mother. When he was home through the day because he was "in between jobs", he constantly screamed at us, "When you dirty a dish, you get in there and wash it!" (Now remember, we didn't have running water.) "If you get it under hot enough water, you don't even need soap...scrub it and it'll dry in a few minutes." He would keep a pot of boiling water on the stove for just this reason.

I look back now and realize that my mother was paralyzed with fear and her emotions were slowly being turned off.

During my elementary years my dad was drunk all the time. When he was home, he and mom fought constantly. When mom left him, my dad would be so upset and he would, of course, try to not drink to get her back...and he trembled...quaked. I've never seen such fear and anxiety in my life. Mom would stand her ground for a few days, and then she would fall back into his arms, seemingly afraid of what might happen to him, hopelessly in love with him, and that would be the end of that.

At that time I saw things through what I now call my "child eyes". Let me explain. If you have ever had a conversation with a three-or four-year-old, you learn quickly that their viewpoint is different from that of an adult. They only see what's directly in their small realm of experience. Everything else is ignored. As adults, we have to guard our more intellectual conversations when we speak to children; points have to be made clearly and simply. Most children can't deal with adult issues because they are not emotionally capable of dealing with them. Most adults struggle with "grown-up" issues so it's all the more wrong to believe a child can.

As you follow this book through the stories of my childhood as well as my adult years, you'll find that until I asked the Lord Jesus to forgive me of my sins and gave my whole life to Him, I saw things as a child would, through my "child eyes". Since I gave my life to Him, I see things through His eyes.

As the scripture states, "When I was a child I saw and thought as a child", but as I began developing my Christian character I put away childish ways of thinking and I now see with my Savior's eyes.

So, with my "child eyes" I saw my home as dirty, my father who drank too much, grew, sold, and smoked pot, and treated his family with no respect and no love. I was angry that mom didn't get her children out of an unsafe environment and for not doing a good enough job to please my father.

Please understand that the reason I feel it's important to know how I viewed my mother and father is not as an excuse for the bad choices I made. But it is an example of how most children of addicted parents feel. No matter what the economic status of the family—that doesn't matter—when alcohol or drugs are involved or any kind of abuse, the question children ask is, "Why don't they just stop what they are doing and take care of me?"

No matter what the economic status of the family—that doesn't matter—when alcohol or drugs are involved or any kind of abuse, the question children ask is, "Why don't they just stop what they are doing and take care of me?"

The answer is, because they don't know the Lord Jesus and understand our loving Father. Through His example I now have direction and clearer sight. This new sight is available to all who call on His name.

a life of lies

A false witness will not go unpunished and he who
breathes out lies will not escape.

Proverbs 19:5 ESV

Because I was embarrassed by how we lived, I coped by developing
a habit of lying. About everything. I learned that if I said something the right way, I could get what I wanted from somebody. I
had no control of the situation at home, no control over the way I
lived, but I could lie and make somebody like me, love me.

My dad was on many drugs—prescription, illegal drugs,
and alcohol cover all the aspects I guess. He was also a truck
driver and took speed to stay awake then took downers because
he'd been on speed so long. His moods were erratic and we
never knew what to expect. Add alcohol to this mix and the
situation was volatile.

We never stayed long enough in one house or town for me
to accumulate enough friends to have a slumber party but the
year I turned nine was *the year*. Yea! A birthday party just for
me!

This was my third grade year of school, and was when I
started to really notice that not all families were like mine...

always fighting…scared…etc. Since dad was away from home most of the time, I assumed he would be gone the night of my party so it would be safe to have friends come to my house. I invited several girls, the house smelled and looked so nice, mom planned games, and we got a great cake.

But dad came home. Drunk.

He was crawling around on his hands and knees, laughing and falling all over himself, pawing at their feet. The girls stood in a circle around him, giggling and hopping up and down like a puppy was after their toes. The girls thought it was so funny, but I was horrified and embarrassed.

That was the only time I ever had a birthday party. It just wasn't worth taking the chance of repeating that scene.

Mom and dad had a big fight that night. I was scared to death that dad would come to my room. I didn't know what might happen. The fear was always there. Always.

He didn't come to my room that night but that birthday was a picture of my daddy. He would come home raging drunk or sloppy, slobbering drunk, falling over things and wouldn't make sense when he talked. Sometimes he would pass out in the middle of the yard and mom would pull at him, tug him up to the house.

About this time in my life my brothers and I started going to First Christian Church. I believe it started with us attending Vacation Bible School. If we had ever gone to church before this, I don't remember, but this would be my first encounter with Christians and the spark of knowledge that there was "something different" out there for me.

When I was about ten we moved about twenty miles away. I don't remember going to church in this new location. Many good things happened in this year but a lot of really bad things began as well. My dad started teaching my brothers the "tricks of the trade" of growing pot.

Before school started in the fall of my fifth grade year, mom told me that if anyone asked about our family to say that my dad didn't live with us. I learned later that dad owed money to a lot of people and they were looking for him. But at the time I thought—*Yes! No one has to know about my dad!*

I loved my dad, but the person he had become because of drugs and alcohol abuse scared me, embarrassed me. Even at ten years of age I wondered what kind of person was I to have those kinds of feelings about my dad? So, I stuffed those emotions deep down and got busy fabricating stories about my life.

> I loved my dad, but the person he had become because of
> drugs and alcohol abuse scared me, embarrassed me.

My teacher did ask about my family and the first lie just slipped out of my mouth without any thought of how I would deal with it. "My father just passed away."

The response made me realize I'd found a way to manipulate my present, my future, the way people looked at me. At that age their pity didn't concern me because with it came a lot of hugs and teachers gave me special treatment. I really wanted to be special.

The lies began to roll off my tongue with no effort at all. I told my teachers, "You know, my mom's struggling 'cause it's hard for her to get through the day." I literally lied my way through all my school years but that year especially.

At the end of the year one of my teachers pulled me aside and said, "I thought you said your father was dead."

I knew by the way she asked that she had learned the truth. But I said, "No, I didn't." I wanted to make her feel like a fool for even asking me.

She said, "You didn't?"

I said, "I don't remember telling you that my father was *dead.* I said he wasn't *with* us."

Of course, I was treated differently then by most of the teachers because they were hurt that I'd lied and they didn't talk to me so much. Then I felt the other children knew that I'd been lying. I guess I thought that I was controlling every single person around me with an individual lie for every circumstance.

When I started the sixth grade I remember feeling I just wanted to hide under a rock all the time. I didn't have many friends, though a friend invited me to a birthday slumber party at her house. I was so impressed by how beautiful her home was. It was just a regular house but it was clean and pretty and felt safe. It was this same year that I learned that Free Lunch meant we were poor and I grew more angry with my parents. I didn't want to be "different".

When dad was unemployed we got food stamps. To get enough money for cigarettes and beer, dad would send us into the store, one by one, with a five dollar food stamp—back then food stamps were in a book with a dollar value on each stamp. I would have to buy a pack of gum or candy, something under a dollar so the store would give me back change. I remember going into the store and looking down at my dirty tennis shoes with holes and thinking—*Why don't they buy me new shoes?*

I took the money to my parents waiting in the car, then each of my brothers went in separately, to get change. Then we'd go to another store and go through the whole routine again. When they had enough cash my dad would go buy his beer and their cigarettes.

During our first year in the house with no running water, The First Christian church bus began coming by for us kids. Mostly it was me that went while my siblings stayed behind. I loved the couple who had the bus ministry. They smelled so nice and spoke kindly to me, and they didn't even care that it took them close to an hour, one way, to get us. Actually, I'm not sure how they found us again, because we had moved so far from our original location, but right then I knew that church was where I wanted to be.

In church is where my life of lies grew. In Sunday School class the teacher took prayer requests, but I couldn't express my fears or needs. If anyone found out that at that very moment my dad was drying pot on screens in our front yard or that one of the sawed-off shotguns he made for someone had just made news when my dad's partner in crime had been arrested and was now plotting to kill a judge! Did they really want to know that

I was afraid to go to sleep at night because I didn't know what might happen to me? Or that I sometimes hid in the closet?

> Did they really want to know that I was afraid to go to sleep at night because I didn't know what might happen to me?

No, I was quite certain that what they wanted to hear had nothing to do with the truth. I was barely surviving it. How would they ever understand?

So, I lied about absolutely everything. I said we had a big house, that we woke up every morning eager to get the day started by feeding all the farm animals and milking the cows. I said each of my siblings and I had our own cow to raise and butcher and invest our savings. I told everyone that my mother was always so happy and had quit smoking and was feeling much better, that my father had a great job where he was the boss.

In reality, my dad only worked half of the time and when he didn't mom "stepped up to the plate". All I could think about was how hurt I was that my dad didn't take care of his family like other dads I met, and how angry I was at my mom for not getting us out of an abusive home.

All year long my lies got bigger and the struggle to keep my two, no three, worlds from colliding became harder. I was afraid that one lie might contradict another and I'd be found out. At church I told them we "had it all together". At home, when mom would ask, I was "learning a lot and had oodles of friends" at school. At school, "My mother is a widow but we're making it just fine."

I lied at school because I was afraid that if they knew how we lived they might notify the authorities and have me removed from home. I was running scared at ten years old!

In the sixth grade I developed the need to be "the best" at whatever challenge was put in front of me. The best at spelling, the best at writing. If I didn't win a talent contest, it was someone else's fault, never mine.

In my eighth grade year I played basketball. I didn't know a whole lot about the game but I did know that my mom had to buy me new socks and new shoes because it was a part of what was required to play. I wanted new shoes and this was a way to get them.

After basketball I got into cheerleading which meant I needed to have new white socks. I didn't get new socks, though. I had my brother's socks with a stripe around the top so I rolled them down to hide it. But I did get new tennis shoes.

My father had lost control of many things in his life and when he failed at something he would lash out at the weakest person around, tear them down to make himself feel better. I began to follow that pattern. I verbally knocked down people who were poor like me but in my mind were different. Everything in my life was self-centered.

All this began to build the basis for my addictions. But the need to feel important, to be something or someone other than myself was there. Not that it's an excuse. I made the choices. Whatever it takes, I thought. Whatever it takes.

My prayer is that some father or mother reading this book will use it as a tool to recognize problems in their children, whatever the age, that can lead to addictions, and as an example of how God's power can rescue and redeem.

I know my life then is not much different from that of many whose parents are on drugs. My father's choices caused my family to live in conditions that are unheard of in modern day. If you're an adult on meth, whether your living conditions are as poor as mine were or not, the heart of your child is at stake. Your child's perception of what is acceptable or normal is *taught to them.* By you. They have no one else to look at. And I guarantee that more than once they have been afraid to go to sleep at night.

> Your child's perception of what is acceptable or normal is *taught to them.*

Now, as an adult who has asked God for His wisdom in sorting through everything that happened either by my parents' choices or my own, I am able to see things clearer. I praise God for new eyes. You see, as I watched my father with my "child eyes", I saw a father who didn't love me enough to stay sober and clean, keep a job, and take care of his little girl like a "good dad" should. Even as an adult I had the same anger and resentment for a long time. Every time I thought of it, it hurt me again.

I grew angrier at my mom as the years passed because even though she cared for me in a nurturing, loving way—no matter how many little things she did—she never touched the things that mattered most, like keeping me safe. Through my "child eyes" I saw my mother so concerned with herself that she didn't take care of me the way a mother should take care of her "little angel". I saw a woman who tolerated the way my father treated her, allowed the way he treated us.

Friends, it is difficult to separate the "in your face" evidence from the facts as seen from a higher perspective. As I grew closer to God, He gave me His point of view, and I was able to see my father as the scared little child who bounced from foster home to foster home, often abused and angry at God and life. He let me see my mother, who lost her father when she was four, and never had a solid understanding of what a good husband and good father looked like. She wanted to love him through his pain and help him get better.

As it stood then, I never told my mother how I felt, how often I blamed her for allowing the hurt in our lives. There were too many years of deception…from all of us. No, this was stuffed down in my secret place in my heart along with many other things. But the lies would eventually catch up with me.

trying to fill the emptiness

The fear of man lays a snare, but whoever trusts in the
Lord is safe.

Proverbs 29:25 ESV

I started drinking when I was fifteen. A friend and I went out
with some boys who had their driver's license and some Boone's
Farm wine. I remember drinking and drinking and getting so
drunk that my lungs felt so full of air...like I was floating. I felt
energized. I felt...free!

I have always been a "high energy" personality anyway, so to
add alcohol to this...well, it just made me silly, and what I had
was a high from the drinking.

While we drove down the highway I tried to open the car
doors. "I'm getting out, I'm getting out." The driver stopped
and I got out and ran, and ran, and ran. They laughed at me
because they were drunk, too, and thought my running was the
funniest thing. For years, when I got drunk I would just run.

I didn't drink that first time because I wanted to escape. I
thought the people who drank were classy people to be with
and I wanted to be with "classy" people. It was obvious to me
that they came from good families and I didn't want to be dif-

ferent so if they drank wine *I* drank wine. If they drank beer *I* drank beer.

Even as I was drinking that night I thought, *What am I doing?* I'd already decided the kind of life I wanted to live. It seemed to me that Christians had better lives. I thought they were happier, they were cleaner, they cared about themselves and about others. I knew that was right and I wanted that; I wanted to live like that.

> Even as I was drinking that night I thought, *What am I doing?*

I remember not wanting to get drunk like that again. But I went to class parties, class dances, and after dancing a while, everybody went out to their trucks to get their beer or wine or whatever so I went with whoever I was with and drank. Pretty soon we left that party and went somewhere else to a bigger party where there was a lot of alcohol. I thought that was the way to popularity and I did want to be popular.

Just before I turned fifteen I had the opportunity to work at a church camp, all summer. A woman who played piano at a church we went to sometimes was going to work at the camp that summer and asked me if I wanted to come and work. I jumped at the chance because I could be away from home for an entire summer!

I went to camp and that woman let me do *everything* on my own! I felt like a real "grownup". It was great! I didn't want to be like her necessarily, but I did take to heart all the things she told me about taking care of myself. She'd tell me something and I'd think, *That makes sense. I'll do that.*

For example, she told me how to take care of my feet. I'd never done that before and they really needed care. At home we went barefoot most of the time and I always had big brown cracks all the way up my heels, and my toenails were rimmed with dirt like you'd taken a marker and outlined them. I hadn't realized that was bad until she told me.

She taught me how to put lotion on my feet and put socks on and sleep like that over night, then scrub my feet really good in the morning. I felt like I was the *cleanest* person.

I had my own money now so I began buying my own clothes. I thought, *I'm going to live differently from everything I've known.* But at the same time I had been drinking all the year before. I thought that every choice I made that didn't agree with my long term goals were just temporary choices…not linking them to the "snowball" that seemed to be forming right in front of my very eyes…and was rolling downhill—fast.

I lost my virginity that same year to someone who meant nothing to me. I was very conscious of how I looked. I'd heard the phrase "A Perfect Ten" so I thought since I wore size ten clothes that meant I was a perfect size. The guy I was dating said, "Well, most girls I date wear a size six."

I said, "What does that mean?"

His answer was, "They're a lot thinner."

I thought if that was what I needed to do to be better then I would lose weight…that's simple enough.

He told me, "Every girl that I've ever dated has been a virgin and they've allowed me to help them learn." By the end of the summer we started having sex…and on my mind was always, *I need to lose weight.*

Later I learned he was a liar and a manipulator. I was so angry about that and thought, *I'm never going to let a man use me again. I'll call the shots.*

But it didn't play out that way. Every time I had sex it was to win the man's affection, to have him say he loved me, to have him say that I was the only one for him, that he couldn't live without me. I did whatever I had to do or say to get their attention. I *needed* that.

Because of my actions, my mother slowly shut her door to me emotionally. She saw what I was doing and was disgusted I'm sure, that her little girl had decided to go down the wrong path. Mom knew who I was becoming and knew that I didn't want to be a part of the family.

By seventeen I was drinking a lot. One night I was out drinking with some new people and we went to a town just over the state line. We'd been drinking Madd Dog and I don't know what else. Typically, if we were not already drunk when we got to our destination, we always knew somebody who had an ID to get into a bar and be served.

I was singing "Amazing Grace", and the guy I was with mentioned he'd been in church all his life but he'd walked away from God. Even drunk as I was, I thought, *I'm not going to be like that. I'm never going to turn away from God.*

But at the same time I didn't have the courage to turn *to* God. As a result, things in my life just got worse and worse. You see, for most teenagers, being popular is very important, but for me I believed it was the only way I had any identity. By the age of seventeen, the biggest goal in life was to seek out anyone who would make me look good, chose men who looked good, or that I could manipulate. I said anything and did anything that made me feel a sense of power, a sense of being in control.

Of course, I was mistaken. Making those kind of compromises is not the way to fill the emptiness inside. But I didn't know that then.

> Making those kind of compromises is not the way to fill the emptiness inside.

At the time, I thought that I was just not walking close to God; that I would live better later—that this phase didn't mean that I was turning away from God, just not to Him. That is the very scary lie that we believe from Satan. We believe that we have time to get it right later if we are not ready now. And even though I am not one to preach fire and brimstone to people, I think that we often forget that scripture is not wishy-washy. God says in First John that we will know who the children of God are and know who the children of the devil are. Those who do not do what is right and do not love one another are *not* of God. It also says that those who *belong* to God do not continue to sin. That does not mean that we are going to be perfect, it simply means that our spirits will be so uncomfortable sinning that we change our ways and we don't go back to the same sin.

That's the truth of scripture that I did not understand then, and had not been taught to that point. I had over a decade of pain to live through still.

searching for "the dream"

I know, O Lord, that the way of man is not in himself,
that it is not in man who walks to direct his steps.

Jeremiah 10:23 ESV

In my senior year of high school mom and dad split up…this time permanently. We moved to town and mom worked tons of hours, managing to just "make ends meet". I didn't know which was worse, seeing mom be so hurt *with* dad or seeing her so hurt *without* him. Both were killing her.

There never seemed to be any joy in our house. I wanted out. I wanted to grow up, fast. I began looking for a place to live where I didn't have to worry about what was happening at home any more. Out of sight out of mind. Avoidance.

A friend and I moved into a trailer. Playing the part of a "grown-up", living on my own, I rarely visited my mom and siblings…my choices were far from mature. I was working at a Golden Corral, waiting tables, and my friend worked at Pizza Hut.

…my choices were far from mature.

Mom didn't come to my graduation and I was so mad at her. Nobody came except the mother of my best friend. She had found out when graduation was and came and took pictures, kind of like family. I didn't invite my mom; I thought she should know, should just be there. But she didn't know; I never told her, so she wasn't there, and I blamed her.

A married friend invited me to move in with her and her husband. Heavy drinking was definitely the norm for me. I'd go out on the weekend and be gone all night. I'd be drunk when I came in and the next day I'd sleep in. I thought I had it made.

I went to work at a little factory with a girl who went partying with me. Some guys and I smoked pot on our lunch break. I'd smoked pot before and never had a problem but this time was different. When we returned to work I couldn't manage to drive the car into a very wide driveway. I thought I was going to miss it and fall into the ditch. My friends said, "You've *got* to stop acting like this. You've got to collect yourself." I was trying but couldn't.

As a result of that experience I decided that if I ever tried pot again it wouldn't be at work, if ever. "Boundaries."

At eighteen I finally realized that my obsession to be the most popular didn't give me the sense of fulfillment I needed. I began searching for something else that would fill the emptiness inside me. I still wanted to be "grown up" so I started living with a boyfriend.

He was also the best friend of Chris, who, it turned out, would become my husband in a little over a year.

Chris came to the house every other night to see my boy-friend so I got to know him. On those nights my boyfriend went out alone to get drunk, Chris and I went out together. As I grew to know him better, my feelings for him changed. Chris seemed to have different values than anyone I had ever met before. He didn't have to have the last word when there was a disagreement even though he was right. He had a confidence that was silent, and his humor was not always crude like every one I knew. He really was different, somehow.

One night when I was out on the town square, in and out of cars talking to people, drinking, I saw Chris and decided to tell him how I felt. He saw me and stopped and I got into his truck. I wasn't sure what his feelings were for me.

"I've got to tell you something. I'm in love with somebody."

"Who is it?" Chris asked.

"Well, it's you."

He stopped. "Get out of my truck."

That wasn't what I expected, but the same values that drew me to him, also made Chris loyal to his friend. Later that night I'd gotten even more drunk when Chris stopped and told me to get into the truck. We drove out to the lake and parked the vehicle and talked.

He said, "I don't know what to do because I think what we're doing is wrong. But I've loved you for two years. I don't know what to do."

We just stood there for what seemed like forever. We cried and talked for a while after that and decided to see where things would lead.

We hid how we felt about one another for a while but it wasn't long before I broke off my former relationship.

After Chris and I started seeing each other openly, we would still be out half the night with our friends, drinking until we were drunk, smoking one cigarette after another. We thought we were so cool. We were eighteen and nineteen years old. Smoking cigarettes, eating mints, spraying cologne. We'd walk into his mom and dad's house thinking they couldn't smell it. We were hiding from ourselves.

We'd stay Saturday night with Chris' folks then go to church with them on Sunday. After church we all ate dinner at his grandpa's house with family. His parents, grandpa, aunts and uncles there around the table. I loved that. After dinner Chris would go sit with the guys and I'd help clean up the kitchen. That was just the most beautiful thing that I had ever experienced. It was my dream to be a part of that.

We continued to party. We also attended church with his family, because "that's what we were supposed to do." Once again, I was creating two different worlds that were bound to collide. I didn't understand the difference between playing a game and having a solid relationship with Christ.

After we'd dated three or four months, Chris and I went to where my ex-boyfriend worked. He would come to church every now and then so when I saw him I said, "We missed you at church today," because I really wanted to play that part.

When we got back into the truck, Chris said to me, "You don't *ever* want to make anybody feel bad for not coming to church. You don't *ever* make yourself above anybody."

I knew that was a part I was playing, but still I said, "What's wrong with that? He *should* be in church!" Again, I was pretending to be somebody I wasn't because I wanted to look good.

Chris and I were married in a traditional wedding in the church where his family attended. I was nineteen years old. My ex (his best friend) was the best man. The church ladies gave us a wedding shower; someone from the church took pictures at the wedding and prepared an album. Another friend made the wedding cake. They didn't know much about me but loved Chris so they all chipped in to make the day special.

My husband told me later that on the day we got married our friends made bets on whether I would divorce him before the year was up. The best man even offered Chris a "get away" car in case he wanted to bolt. I had that kind of reputation and I had only myself to blame. At the time, of course, I blamed everyone else.

We were barely nineteen years old and I had no idea what my dream was. I thought that my husband should have the responsibility of making my dreams come true.

> We were barely nineteen years old and I had no idea
> what my dream was.

If a couple has committed themselves to God, this process of growing up together can be beautiful. Watching one another love Jesus and His ways is so attractive, and believing that each of you are directed by a faithful Father takes the mistrust out of any relationship. On the opposite hand, to grow into a party scene together typically adds into the union every tool available to rip the marriage apart.

It is only by God's mercy and grace and our individual decisions to make Him Lord of our lives that saved our marriage. We thank Him for this daily.

lured away

But each person is tempted when he is lured and enticed
by his own desire.

James 1:14 ESV

After Chris and I married, I got a job at a pharmacy and soon a second job waiting tables at a local restaurant. That's a lot of working hours for a person who at the same time would stay up drinking most of the previous night. In addition to being tired all the time, I was still very conscious of how I looked and thought I needed to lose weight. A girl I worked with introduced me to Mini Thins. She said she took six at a time and I thought, *You're an addict!*

That first time I took three Mini Thins, 25 mg each, I didn't feel tired any more! As a bonus, I didn't think about being awkward around anybody and I could talk about anything! I thought, *These make me so social!*

The pills gave me such energy, but the crash was hard and fast. I'd be in the pharmacy doing the billing for Medicaid patients and falling asleep while standing at the counter. My first thought wasn't that I should have slept the night before, but instead I thought I need more Mini Thins.

I never went into anything gradually, just went into it full force. In just weeks I was addicted, buying Mini Thins at a local convenience store and taking a hand full at a time.

We were still going out and drinking every night. To stay awake at the pharmacy, I swallowed half the contents of a bottle in the morning. Before long I was terminated from the pharmacy and began working split shifts at a restaurant. By the time I reached the second half of my shift at five-thirty or six, I was exhausted so I'd take the rest of the bottle.

Fifty Mini Thins in the morning, fifty in the evening. A full bottle a day. I remember thinking, *I can wait tables and support this "habit"*. But I didn't want Chris to know I had this little problem. If I didn't have my Mini-Thins, I had my Sudafed back-up—six, seven or eight Sudafed at a time. My addiction to Mini Thins traveled with me for years, on and off…mostly on.

My addiction to Mini Thins traveled with me for years, on and off…mostly on.

At one time I even thought about having a psychiatric evaluation, not because I thought I was crazy or depressed, but because I had a friend who was on antidepressants and she *loved* them. She said they were the "best invention in pharmaceuticals" because she finally had enough energy and felt so good while she was going to school to be a respiratory therapist.

I didn't go. That was the grace of God before I even knew He was working in my life. Who knows where prescription drugs would have taken me. But I continued to abuse Mini Thins for many years. No matter what drug I had tried at whatever time in my life, I kept my bottle ready for back up…daily. Even through my addiction to meth.

Friends who party know other friends who party, and before one knows what is happening, the circle of friends will lead a person to yet another drug. Soon we were introduced to pot, which was a first for my husband, and for myself, a boundary that I had previously placed was moved, again.

Someone brought a bag of pot for us to try. We said we'd try it but told ourselves we'd *never* buy it. We'd *never* spend our money on drugs. Meanwhile, Chris' drinking grew worse.

Many times when a person begins using any kind of drug, it's free. The friends will "share". They themselves want to have "fun" and subconsciously don't want to party alone, so the drug is simply offered. Soon the "sharing" is not so good anymore. If a new friend keeps bumming drugs, it's not cool. Soon, some find that it is beneficial to do something to help the dealer out in order to receive drugs for free. We found that we could have free pot if Chris would help manicure. Very soon, Chris was in the middle of the whole scene.

Chris was afraid of being discovered in the pot patch pulling up huge plants—being in the middle of piles and piles of big plants on both sides. But at the same time it was exhilarating. He was just as much addicted to the adrenaline rush as he was from the drugs.

We smoked pot for perhaps a year before we began partying with another crowd. Through this new crowd, Chris was introduced to meth.

If you're smoking pot, in your house or at someone else's house, more than likely you're going to end up being associated with meth, too. For us there was a progression of addictions—alcohol, free pot/buying pot/growing pot (smoking pot on weekends then smoking every day), coke, meth. The progression.

One morning on the way home from the convenience store where I bought my daily supply of Mini Thins, I wrecked my car. I was trying to get the bottle open, not paying attention to the road, and I ran into the pillars of an overpass. Fortunately, I wasn't hurt but the car was wrecked. Chris had to take me to work in his truck which created a problem for me. To keep him from knowing how hooked I was on Mini Thins, I'd take the truck and go to the convenience store before Chris got up. I don't know what the clerk at the store thought. I bought bottles and bottles and hid them because I was afraid I wouldn't have enough.

Then our lives took another turn. Chris was driving me to work one morning when I told him to pull over and I vomited at the side of the road. I thought, *I need to cut back.* Duh.

The nausea was there every day, and I was hungry *all the time.* I knew that with taking Mini Thins I shouldn't be hungry, and since I was waiting tables I shouldn't have been gaining weight, but I was.

Finally it dawned on me to take a pregnancy test. When the results were positive, I dumped the whole bunch of hoarded Mini Thins. Just threw them in the trash.

Amazingly enough, I was still able to go to work and to function.

Telling Chris I was pregnant didn't change his lifestyle. Just mine. He was drinking, still going out and partying on the weekends, but I decided I wasn't going to drink or smoke any more. I wanted to take care of my body. But I was working with a girl who was also pregnant and she said, "Oh, two cigarettes a day won't hurt the baby. You can have up to three a day." As crazy as that sounds, I believed her.

So I started smoking a cigarette on break. Oh, the hit on my lungs! Oh, I just wanted another one. I'd go to bed at night and I'd have had three cigarettes but I didn't think that was too bad. I thought, *I'm not a bad person.*

I smoked pot a couple of times because I just wanted to do it. I would laugh, then suddenly I wasn't laughing any more. I knew smoking pot could hurt my baby, so why was I doing it? It just didn't seem *that* bad.

I would laugh, then suddenly I wasn't laughing any more.

That's the trap. It doesn't seem so bad.

I was angry at Chris all the time, but at the same time I was joyful because of the baby I was carrying. I carried around a chart that showed the baby's size and I would tell everybody, "She's *this* big," and "She's got eyes," and on and on.

I was determined to be the very *best* mom. I was not going to make any mistakes. I would teach my child how to learn and teach her about proper hygiene. I would show her it was important to keep her toys clean. My home would be the total opposite of what my home had been growing up.

Tabatha's birth was an incredible experience. Five hours of labor, maybe thirty minutes of hard labor. Not a big deal. And it felt *awesome* when she slipped into the world. It was the most marvelous feeling, the most beautiful thing in my life at that point.

The day Tabby was born I resolved again to be the very best mother. I was never going to do *anything* wrong.

We hadn't chosen a pediatrician at the time because we were "self-pay". We didn't have insurance or Medicaid, so we had made payments monthly to the doctor and had decided to use the hospital's staff pediatrician, because of the expense of retaining one before she was born. The pediatrician on staff came to my room after she examined Tabatha for her newborn evaluation.

"Initial examination indicates your baby has Down Syndrome."

The doctor spoke in a very dry, very matter of fact voice and I didn't understand what she meant. I sat there in that hospital room as our lives were changing drastically.

"She has the downward sloping eyes, flattened nose, no muscle tone, small, low-set ears, the down turn to her mouth."

This doctor was talking about my baby like there was something horribly wrong with her.

My mind wouldn't accept what I was hearing—*But that's the most beautiful baby in the whole nursery! I don't believe what you're saying!*

I didn't understand. The doctor repeated the facts then finally she said, "Corky", the character's name from a television show about a young man with Down Syndrome. I'd watched that show. I finally began to understand what the doctor was saying.

While the doctor talked, Chris sat there and I could see him; he just...left. Mentally, emotionally.

"How sure are you?" I finally asked.

"Ninety-nine point nine percent."

"How can you be a hundred percent sure?"

"I want you to come back in two days and we'll draw blood for Karytype testing. If it comes back that she has an extra chromosome, three copies of chromosome 21, called trisomy 21 (normally a person has two copies) then we'll know for certain."

I began to think, *What if? What if she is? What if she isn't? What if?*

I was angry. Angry at the pediatrician for even thinking something was wrong with my baby. Every time I looked at Tabatha I told myself there was *no* sign of "Down Syndrome" in my child. I would not even use the name Down Syndrome. I called it IT.

Before we got the test results back, I was laying on our water bed, my feet dangling off the end of the bed, and I was talking to the God of the Universe. I knew that what I had been doing in my life was wrong. I thought maybe I was being punished for straying from Him and living a life that didn't include Him. Of course, at that time in my life, I didn't understand God's heart. It's not to punish us, but to bless us; to draw us to His side; to love us. Tabby was and is a precious gift from a perfect God...that is the true picture...wow.

But at this time in my life all I understood to say to Him was, "God, just take my life and let her be normal. Just take me."

I *meant* it. And I knew that He heard me.

There are those times that you know the conversation between you and God is as if He is standing right next to you, looking you in the eyes, listening to you intently. This was one of those times. I knew that day, that if I died, I would go to hell. In my heart, I knew it beyond a shadow of a doubt. I didn't understand His plan for me. There are many of you that are still talking to God and know that you are not right with Him. Waiting for Him to wave his holy wand and fix all the things in your life that need fixing. You are waiting for Him to prove that He is for you and is never going to leave you to stand in this life alone. He is speaking to you now and telling you one thing. Surrender. Surrender your life and your desires for His life and His desires. Then and only then are you able to experience what freedom feels like. It is so *restful,* so right.

God was speaking to me then, but I didn't listen. Not yet.

the addiction

Then desire when it has conceived gives birth to sin, and
sin when it is fully grown brings forth death.

James 1:15 ESV

We got the test results back and it was positive, of course,
Tabatha had IT. Down Syndrome.

After we brought Tabatha home I received a call from a nurse
at the hospital who had a little boy with Down Syndrome.

"I heard about you and about your baby. I know what you're
about to go through. I wanted to call and give you some encouragement, start giving you some facts."

I didn't know what to say. She sent me copies of books and
information about Down Syndrome so I could start educating
myself.

At this point Chris started drinking even more. I can't say
he was a bad father. He loved Tabatha. He would lay on the bed
or couch with her on his chest and talk to her for hours.

I made sure she had physical therapy and everything necessary for her special needs. I never gave Chris the opportunity
to take part in that. I'd never say, "*We* need to…" It was always,
"*I* need to…"

My need to control everything let Chris off the hook for handling the hard stuff. It allowed him to go deeper and deeper into his addictions. I picked up the "bottle" again; the bottle wasn't alcohol but my pills weren't any better. I went back to buying Mini Thins at the local convenience store. My reasoning was that I needed them to get some things done, get some things organized.

> My need to control everything let Chris off the hook for handling the hard stuff.

Just weeks after Tabatha was born, we picked up our old life. Friends started coming to our house and we drank every night. I began smoking again, telling myself I'd only do it when I drank wine, or only drink wine when I smoked. During the day I was the "perfect" mother but it was a whole different world when Tabatha closed her eyes at night.

Pot was available in abundance again…it was harvest time. I justified my use by saying I wouldn't do it until Tabatha went to sleep at night. But after a while I needed something to get up in the morning, then something to get through the middle of the day. The snowball began to roll downhill. Fast.

Pretty soon my boundary was to make sure that Tabby was never in the room with me when I smoked pot. I put her in the dining room in her swing, just far enough away that she didn't hear or see anything because I didn't want to be such a terrible mom. I was justifying my addictions. I was using pot as if I didn't have a child to be responsible for.

Then Chris brought home a bag of meth.

The night he brought home the first bag of meth I had two equal feelings to deal with.

Why would he bring that into our home when we have so much to deal with?

On the other hand, I got to try a new drug: one that after the very first hit had me, and I was addicted.

Before I go on I want to tell you a story that our pastor told one Sunday morning only a couple of years ago. He explained the process of how a hunter captures a wolf in the very cold regions. The hunter will take his knife and soak and freeze blood on the blade until the blood covered blade is quite thick with this. He then takes the knife and securely places it in the ground, blade up. A wolf will smell the blood and be drawn to the knife. As he starts licking the knife, a gluttony for the taste of blood overcomes him and he is not aware of the moment when he is no longer licking the blood off of the blade, but is in fact, now drinking his own blood. All the hunter has to do is wait until the wolf dies. His own desire killing him.

At the time of my first experimentation, I didn't think of the years that would be devoured. I didn't understand how the gluttony would take over, but it did. I tried desperately to juggle being a good mom, with the overwhelming need for the drug. Again, two worlds colliding.

At three-months-old Tabatha started vomiting frequently. By four and a half months she was vomiting all the time. Everything she ate came right back up. I took her to the pediatrician and we learned that she had a serious heart defect, one that required immediate surgery or she wouldn't survive. Fifty percent of Down Syndrome babies have heart problems. With Tabby, no murmur had been detected earlier because there had been equal pressure in her heart as the blood flowed in and out.

She was scheduled for surgery. We were scared. We waited and worried through the surgery, scared, blaming ourselves. But she came through the surgery. I stayed at the hospital while Tabby recovered. Chris had to be at work every day.

My thoughts should have been all consumed with taking care of Tabby, but an equal force pulled at me. I needed something...something to deal with everything. Chris justified his growing addiction to meth with this same reasoning. "I need to work overtime." Mostly we needed the drug's ability to numb emotions with which we were both *not* dealing.

Before I go any farther, please understand that it has been my experience that most mothers and fathers who are addicted to this horrible drug hate it! They hate what it is doing to their bodies, their minds, yet they feel trapped. They feel hopeless; that's how I felt...hopeless.

We must get the proper attitude toward this addiction that is destroying our homes. Loved ones are overcome with so many emotions that they, too, are drawn into the pit. Mothers and fathers of addicts are disgusted, ashamed, afraid, and angry. At the same time their hearts are ripped apart as they see their son or daughter hit emotional peaks of highs and lows. While a person is on meth, their ability to feel or recognize their own emotions is diminished. A numbness sets in as soon as the drug hits your bloodstream.

Mothers and fathers of addicts are disgusted, ashamed, afraid, and angry.

To an addict of many years, numbness is no longer just a desire. It becomes a need. Without the drug, emotions not only surface but they rush to the surface all at once. They overwhelm. You use in order *not* to feel.

With pot, pills, and meth, we were able to keep our "high" going on an almost continual basis. They were always available in abundance and always in the pockets of our friends. And our "friends" were always at our house.

At first I could stay up for two, three days at a time and it wasn't that big of a deal. At first it just made me feel—I don't know—good. It made me feel social. It gave me confidence. I could be so open with people, open about Tabatha and about all the appointments I had with her and everything that was going on with her.

When she was a baby and a small child, Tabby would look into my eyes all the time. Now she has an eye avoidance, but when she was a baby she didn't. When I talked to her I felt embarrassed because I had just taken a bunch of speed or I had smoked pot or I had drunk alcohol…so I would look away. Maybe she learned the eye-avoidance from my example. I'll never know for sure.

Chris and I sank deeper and deeper into addiction. One day I'd taken I don't know how many Mini Thins, then meth on top of that.

Suddenly I couldn't take a deep enough breath. I sat in the kitchen, trying to breathe.

"I need to relax. Just relax."

I tried to listen to my favorite rock station but I couldn't tune it in. All I heard was my heartbeat, loud in my ears. Thump-thump, thump-thump.

Finally I got enough breath but for almost a week every time I tuned into that station there was only the sound of a heartbeat. Thump-thump, thump-thump, thump-thump…and it increased in tempo and volume until I couldn't stand it. I would be in the car and I would feel locked inside my skin. Just…skin crawling.

I thought that heartbeat was a message. I knew that God was real. I knew that I should not even be alive because of all the speed that I was putting in my body. I thought God was trying to tell me I was going to die.

I know many people that tell me how many times they felt the same feeling of not being able to breath deep enough, or fearful of the overdose of speed, and some of them did overdose to the point of a blackout as their eyes rolled back in their heads. Yet they are still using. My prayer is that they will hear this as loudly as I heard those heartbeats, and turn to God for life.

At that time though, I didn't listen. Not really.

losing control

Be sober minded; be watchful. Your adversary, the devil, prowls around like a roaring lion, seeking someone to devour.

1 Peter 5:8 ESV

Chris has always been mechanically inclined. Early in our marriage he was a gas engine mechanic. That didn't pay enough to support a family so he took a job with another company as their truck mechanic, then as a gutter installer.

One night Chris was leaving the house with a friend, and at the time I was trying to stop using meth.

"Why are you leaving?"

Chris just looked at me. "Because we're addicted. We need to support our habit."

I thought, *What? We're not addicted!*

But he was telling the truth. He was angry at me.

"You want to go out and get it? You can't. I'm the connection so I have to go."

That hit hard!

Because of circumstances at his work, Chris was called in for a drug test, and he refused to take it. He was a good employee and his supervisor was surprised at Chris' response; so was I, for now he was without a job. I watched as we started to become more like the people we hung out with…without a job because of the inability to take a simple urinalysis.

Chris was now dealing drugs, and that's how we supported our habit for quite a few months. We had literally hoards of people in and out of our house all the time to buy their meth. I kept telling him to get a job. The people who came into our home to buy drugs told him to get a job.

One of our friends, who didn't do drugs but drank, said, "You know, you don't always like the things you do but you have to take care of your family. So get out there and get a job."

Chris respected this person so he started job hunting. He applied for a position with a diesel shop but he was scared to go in because he had no solid diesel experience, but he knew a lot and had worked on a lot of diesel powered implements. To get the job he had to take a physical…and he had to have a drug test.

In order to pass the drug test, Chris bought a chemical altering medication, available at most "head shops", to skew the results. It took a while but it actually worked. The lab knew something was wrong with his sample and sent it to another lab. We assumed the lab could tell it had been altered but they couldn't tell from what, so they couldn't say Chris had drugs in his system. They had to return the test as negative for drugs.

We were both using meth the whole time, although Chris had slowed down considerably in order to take the urinalysis and—surprisingly—he got the job.

About this same time, we met a big time dealer who was looking for a good middle man he could work with. That was Chris.

Our life was deteriorating; our marriage was in trouble. The more meth we did, the more we fought. People who used were in and out of the house, while our daughter slept in the other room. We were smoking, using meth, watching porn movies (which is typical of that world).

Our life was deteriorating; our marriage was in trouble.

The more meth we used, the more we watched those kind of movies. I began dressing very provocatively. It was like I was transforming into the images I was watching. It was hard to keep my "mommy" world and my "other" world from colliding. Finally I woke up one day and said, "That's it. No more." I looked at Tabby and made my choice. No more meth.

But Chris was The Dealer and he thought it was too late for him. After all, how *do* you get out of a position like that when some of the people you deal with carry weapons, and most are terribly paranoid about who was going to quit and "snitch them out".

At the time we were living in a duplex and our landlord was the town mayor. His wife had just finished law school and worked for the prosecuting attorney. We knew we were being watched. Our landlord warned us that we were associating with people who were under investigation and if we were doing something we shouldn't, then we'd better stop...now! We ignored the warning.

Like my parents had done, Chris and I separated several times. Any time we split up, Chris did tons of meth, then he'd get into a raw rage. One night, I was scared to be at the house so I went to my brother's house and he returned with me. When we got back, Chris was in the house and we were locked out. My bother and I banged on the back door.

"You *will* let me in this house!" I yelled. "This is *my* home! This is *not* your home!"

"You're gonna have to come in after me. You can have the house but you're gonna have to come in after me."

Well, my brother is a pretty hefty guy. Not large, but he's muscled. So he broke in the door. When we walked in, Chris was on the phone with the police. High as a kite himself, but he was thinking, *I got her on something this time.* We were both always trying to put each other in jail.

The police came and they questioned both of us. I told them my side of the story, that Chris was strung out on drugs, that he was trying to mess with me.

"You were the one that did the breaking and entering, and your brother *did* hit Chris with a ball bat. It's been reported before that he's been harassing you, and we have the witness of other people, but you're the one who forcibly gained entry. And now there's the assault to deal with."

I could hardly believe what I was hearing.

The officers weighed everything then arrested me for domestic violence. They arrested Chris, too, but I was shocked that they arrested me!

I was crying as they put me in the patrol car. *I can't believe I'm going to jail!*

> *I can't believe I'm going to jail!*

I was put in a cell with a woman who was pacing back and forth, talking to herself.

"It wasn't my fault, I just went to this house. I wasn't *in* the house. I wasn't with that meth, I was just in the car but I had to go pee so I got up to go pee and I had to go into the house to go pee. I was just in the house to pee when the cops busted in. I had no idea who these people were—"

I thought, *Is she delusional? She can't even talk to make sense!* It had been a few weeks since I had taken any drugs or drunk alcohol, so I was clear enough to think, *Can't she see? Doesn't she understand that what she's saying is the most stupid story? And she's going to stick with this?*

There I was. In jail. With this woman.

Chris and I were in the same jail but he was in his cell thinking, *She's giving it up. She's telling all our contacts. She's gonna be a rat and I'm going to be killed because my wife is telling all about our contacts.*

He was furious with me.

I hadn't said anything about our drug contacts or anything. I thought, *I'm in this jail cell and I'm just going to be here as long as necessary then go home.*

I was sitting on this hard bench of a bed—a bench hanging from the wall—and had only this teeny-tiny blanket to cover up with. I was curling up on a bare braided metal bench, wearing Capri's so half my legs were bare, trying to cuddle up to a cold wall with a tiny blanket.

I was even looking to the other woman for counsel on how to get warm because I could see that she had been there before. She had wrapped her blanket tight around all of her body and kind of scrunched it up, gathered it into a ball, like she'd done it a hundred times. So that's what I did, too. I was officially a part of "that world".

I was furious at myself and I hated Chris more that day than any day before.

Two men came into the cell. I saw DEA (Drug Enforcement Agency) on their jackets.

Oh! Oh! They're gonna talk to me!

But they went to the other woman. They sat on the narrow bunk with her.

"Stop this. You don't have to be in this mess any more. Tell us what we need to know so you can be done with this. There are rehab programs…"

I thought they were so kind as they tried to counsel her to get out of it. They seemed genuinely concerned about this woman getting off meth. I felt they were in it to get people off meth and to get other people who didn't want to get out, put behind bars.

The woman wouldn't budge off her story.

"I don't know what you're talking about. I have a story and I'm gonna stick to it. I don't know what you're talking about."

If I ever was busted would I do that?

I probably would have. I'd have found a story and stuck to it. Not divulged any information because that's a *big* topic when you're in a house and everybody is waiting for the drug dealer to show up.

"What would you do if the cops stopped you?"

"Well," someone would say, "I'd get out of the car and I'd run and I'd throw the drug out as I ran. I'd never let them catch me, and if they caught me I'd *never* mention your name. No way. I'd never mention any names."

It was a big deal. You had to rely on one another. Solid *trust*. Oh brother, what a misrepresentation of the word! There was *no* trust. It was all lies and deceit and narcs everywhere you looked. But everybody always said, "You can trust me."

My family was trying to get me out of jail but I had to serve the full twenty-four hours. Chris' dad had retained an attorney and he was released earlier.

This was a wake-up call, but a few years later I was still in the middle of my addictions.

When I got out of jail I swore I would never do drugs again.

I saw Chris from time to time when he came to see Tabby and finally we'd both had enough of being apart.

"We just need to silence all the voices from friends and family," he said, "and get back together."

I loved him so much and hated all of the stuff that took us to this point that I agreed. We needed to be together. But, we had no money so we moved in with Chris' folks.

The boss of the shop where Chris worked regularly reported to the main shop that was located in a city about an hour's drive away. He reported that Chris was doing several things wrong and management needed to let him go. When Chris became aware of this conversation, he drove to the main office to talk to the boss himself.

He explained to the manager that he was a good worker, that he felt that he could prove this and wanted to be given a chance.

Now this is a God thing. Even though we were working for the enemy (Satan) at the time, God laid things out to get us to move. Even *then* God was laying out a path for us.

"There's a temporary position here," the boss told Chris, "that I need filled. You come here and we'll just see if any of this is true."

When Chris proved he was a solid worker, he was asked to transfer permanently.

We were living with Chris' folks so he was driving the seventy miles one way to work every day. I had stopped using meth but Chris had not, and I knew he was getting some on the way to and from work. I had labeled meth abuse as "living wrong," but was taking Sudafed by the hand full. There was no place to hide my Mini Thins but I had my boxes of Sudafed in the medicine cabinet. I said I needed it for my allergies. I was still lying to myself.

Chris and I still fought all the time. One evening I'd prepared a large meal for the entire family but he was late getting home. We waited, then finally sat down to eat. When Chris finally came home I was mad and met him outside to tell him about having prepared the meal and that we'd already eaten.

We walked into the woods to talk.

"I know what you're doing and I'm going to all the dealers and tell them I'm going to narc on them," I told him. "And when I die (I knew they'd kill me) then you'll know how much I love you and want you out of this." I just so desperately wanted to make him quit.

When a person wants to change someone because they see that what the person is doing is hurting that person, they often scramble for the best way to manipulate them, thinking that they are doing the situation justice. When we do this, however, we are only making matters worse. To try to control someone, first of all is not fair on them. They are not going to turn to God, because you have set yourself up to be the deity of their lives. Secondly, it will place you in the middle of the pit right along with them, and now there are two people that need to be rescued. Yuck.

> To try to control someone, first of all is not fair on them.
> They are not going to turn to God, because you have set
> yourself up to be the deity of their lives.

Of course I didn't tell anyone that and his usage continued.

We had to move to get near Chris' job, so we hocked many of the large items from our home, and rented a motel room in yet another new city for a couple of weeks while we found a place to live in that area.

It took two weeks to find a place we could afford. Back home we'd rented a nice duplex for $300 a month but there was no way we could find anything comparable in the new town. We were finally able to rent a little trailer with an add-on for $300 a month.

I started using meth again.

living in darkness

The way of the wicked is like deep darkness; they do not
know over what they stumble.

Proverbs 4:19 ESV

Living with a meth addiction is living in a dark, dark world.
For years we put towels or sheets over our windows during the
daytime so light wouldn't come in. A lot of addicts do that. You
want it to be night all the time. You live for the night time.

At night we kept the windows covered because we didn't
want anybody to see the lights. We were up all night, and we
lived in darkness all the time. I was like a mole, blinded by
daylight.

I was like a mole, blinded by daylight.

During this period, we watched as our friends, some of
whom were from a position of "good standing", in terms of
family and wealth, were taken to a humiliating low. Many are
still there today. Meth has its claws in them...destroying them
and their families.

Life got very dark for me. Tabatha would be in her bedroom asleep, the house would be full of the kind of people that I

swore would never be around my kids, and they were right there in our living room.

Sometimes we would go to someone's house to wait for the dealer to show up. We'd wait three or four hours thinking that he'd be there any minute; any minute this person is going to show up.

One night we were waiting at a house to buy drugs when a young man who was a friend of my little brother came in. I was afraid he would tell him about seeing me. I never wanted my family to know *anything* of what I did. We'd grown up with my dad's addictions and alcoholism and hated it. I didn't want my family to have to watch me go through what we had seen my dad do, and I was so embarrassed.

So there I was, in the corner covering up as much of me as I could, slinking back, waiting. You'd think we would have left, but we wouldn't. We thought, *any minute the dealer's gonna be here.* Any minute...

We sank deeper into the darkness of addictions. I remember being so drunk one night that I lost all ability to get up from the floor. I had been awake for three plus days on meth and had decided that I would "have a few to wind down," so I drank. I don't know how much. As I tried to get up, I remember pawing at the floor and laughing uncontrollably. I tried to roll over to get up and again was stuck like glue to the floor, and could only half recall what I had done the night before.

So much like my father when he was drunk.

That period of my life is not something I like to remember. We were using meth daily and had been for quite some time. Our decisions were beyond poor…they were leading us straight to Hell. But I tell about it here because there are a lot of people who might think Chris and I haven't done as much as they've done, or it wasn't as bad for us as it is for them. If that is you, and you are thinking, *You don't know what I've done. How could God forgive me?*

God will allow me to say…I've been there. I've thought the same thing. But He's forgiven me. He'll do the same for you. I can "recall" those times of disgrace, but the emotional attachment is no longer there. God is so faithful, so merciful, to give us peace.

One by-product of meth addiction is that it turns your God-given sexuality into something horrible. Meth heightens the sex drive. Men and women both want more and more of the drug because of that effect it has on them. The majority of people we met were involved in something morally and sexually degrading. There were the pornographic videos, infidelity, and adultery that seemed okay because of the effect of meth and the videos we watched over and over. Chris and I went to strip clubs together and I watched women take off their clothes for my husband and I thought nothing of it.

Meth brings a numbness over you; the drug in your body and the endorphins release a *strong* sex drive. It's a hunger that you have to feed. And once you start feeding that hunger at point A, you're going to end up at the very end of the alphabet.

You *will* feed it more and more and even at the end you need something more. That's something nobody wants to talk about. Life becomes a living hell.

I guess I should have been more jealous. He was never unfaithful to me—I mean, not without me being there—but I was.

It grieves my heart but that first night, being with someone else seemed okay to me. Not "okay-okay", but that numbness that comes over you when you're on meth makes you not think about the right or wrong of things. You just...*need*. It's a part of the world you live in.

The Bible tells us that when you start sinning it demands more and more and more. Once you have a taste of it, it takes a little more to satisfy you, then a little more, then a little more, until pretty soon it's just an uncontrollable hunger and you're looking for anything to fill that desire.

Even though Chris and I both hated each other for what had happened—I hated him for even asking me to do it, and he hated me for doing it—pretty soon we were talking about being with someone else again. The more you do meth the more you think, "I hate who I am but this *is* who I am."

> The more you do meth the more you think, "I hate who I am but this *is* who I am."

We may have hated what we did but we continued to watch the movies, we still talked about being with other people. That was now a part of our intimate life. Most addicts we were around talked about and did the very same thing. It's a part of that world.

So we put those things in the little *I Hate You* harbor spot and kept it there.

Years later, after Chris and I were saved, we went to a marriage conference at our church. The speaker, Tommy Nelson, talked about trust, intimacy, and faithfulness. My husband knew what I was thinking and *I* knew what *I* was thinking. That night I just cried and cried a lifetime of tears and said over and over, "I'm *so* sorry."

"We've got to leave it there. I forgave you for that a long time ago," my husband said. "We've got to leave it there. I'm sorry, too."

And we were just done with that.

The Bible tells us to forget what is behind and press on toward our goal which is Christ Jesus. We're now devoted to living for a wonderful God who forgives all and washes away every sin, and every pain. That's the grace of God.

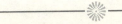

But while we were still in the worst part of our addictions, Chris felt hopeless. His hair began falling out, leaving perfectly round bald patches on the side of his head. He had the same perfectly round bald spots on his face where his beard grew. His feet were scabby and blistered at the same time. They were rotting.

He couldn't get up for work without doing a "bump" of meth, then doing another at work, and more when he got home. The music we listened to became darker. Songs that said there was no hope. Songs that talked about death and unforgiveness.

We felt that there was no way we could be forgiven for the things we had indulged in.

There was no joy in our house at all. It was like blackness had set itself up in our hearts. We stopped going to public places where we might have to talk with someone. I avoided conversations with teachers and grew distant from our daughter.

She was the most pure thing I could imagine, and I was disgusted with myself for even standing next to her innocence.

Paranoia about everything and everyone had set in. I was literally jumping around in my own skin, scared to move and scared to live.

It says in the Bible that where there's light there is no darkness. Meth and the world it represents is the darkness of addiction in which Satan imprisons people. The only way to break out is to turn on the light. Invite Christ Jesus in, for He is light. He is waiting to break the chains of addiction. "He is light and in Him there is no darkness." But we were so immersed in the darkness of meth addiction we couldn't breathe, couldn't see any way out. It wasn't until a few years later that we found our way out. You don't have to wait that long and go through more pain that comes with living in darkness. God is waiting. We just had to find the courage to turn toward the light, but, unfortunately, we chose to travel a dark road for a while longer.

> Meth and the world it represents is the darkness of addiction in which Satan imprisons people.

This is a part of this story of my past that I explained in the introduction that I would rather not say out loud, let alone put on paper for the world to read, but it is something that is so dark that most who come off of the drug don't want to have to deal with. God will never make us deal with things that we are not capable of handling, but I feel that God will allow me to say this is an area that can be a foothold for Satan. If we don't deal with the darkest points, in order to give as well as receive forgiveness, then it is usually something that will pop up and haunt our new lives in Christ. I can say boldly that I am free from this bondage, because I believed God when He told me to forgive all people involved with this point of my life. I forgave, and now am able to freely receive His forgiveness for this. God is so faithful.

the darkness grows deeper

For everyone who does wicked things hates the light and does not come to the light, lest his deeds should be exposed.

John 3:20 ESV

Chris' father died at age fifty-five from heart failure, and for a while we went to see his mom every weekend. She still lived out on a farm where the house was heated with wood in the winter. It was a big system where hot water pipes went underneath the floor. The big stove was out in a shed and had to be stocked full every morning before she went to work. My husband and his brother built a lean-to and they cut wood every weekend to make sure there was enough stacked for the week.

We'd leave Tabatha with Chris' mother all weekend. I knew it was wrong but we used his mom as a babysitting service and a place to stay because all our drug connections were in that area.

On Sunday she'd take Tabatha to church but I didn't go. I'd say, "I'm going to stay here and help Chris." That gave me another chance to have another day, a few hours anyway, so I could do another line or whatever. Running from my responsibilities of being a mother.

I'd go to pick up Tabatha and my face was totally picked apart, scabs all over. His mother had to know something was wrong with us, but she didn't acknowledge it for a long time because she wanted to do the right thing for Tabatha.

Finally she confronted us.

"Something's wrong. You guys are being weird. I want you to be here but you stay a couple of hours then you're gone all night. Then the next day you're working and we never get to see each other and I'm always watching Tabatha...all weekend."

Chris snapped back at her, "Don't worry about it. If you're upset about babysitting, then Tabatha won't be coming here any more."

The person I relied on to always say the right thing said the opposite of what I had in my head, the opposite of what he was supposed to say. His mom just took it.

"Okay, okay. I just want to see you...With your dad gone..."

I watched her sink into a shell. She just needed somebody so badly. Whatever she could do for us, even if it drained every amount of energy she had, she would do. We were using my family the same way...but we had lived this life as children... and had learned, *Don't talk about it!* I truly had taken over the role of my father.

> ...but we had lived this life as children...and had learned,
> *Don't talk about it!*

Then the company Chris worked for began performing random drug tests. For a while we thought that Chris was just lucky that he didn't have to take one, but the first one he took came back positive. Typically, if an employee had a positive drug test, they were automatically fired. No second chances. But they let Chris have a second chance because he had proven to be good worker.

Chris was aware that while on probation with the company during this period that he would have to undergo a monthly urinalysis. Two or three months went by without being called in for a drug test. He was drinking this stuff to alter his urinalysis, keeping it in his truck just in case he was tested.

His mom was selling the farm and we were "helping" her— we were still partying in the shed at night while she was watching the girls (by this time we had our second daughter). We were at the farm when the company called and told Chris that he needed to come in to work early. What happened was he was sent to the drug testing facility. Chris was out of the "chemical altering" drink so he had to take the test without it. The chances are slim to none that you can manage to do this drug and pass a urinalysis. That's why most people who are doing meth cannot keep a job.

Chris failed the drug test and was let go. But even that didn't open his eyes, didn't open my eyes. We KNEW, we *KNEW.*

Present friends, friends and mentors from our new life, have asked about our life in the drug world.

"What did you do? Did you just sit around at somebody's house and do drugs all the time?" (*Our new friends just can't relate*—Praise God!)

"That's the crazy thing of it," Chris has told them. "You don't *do* drugs the whole time. You spend more time *looking* for the drug, *waiting* for the drug, *creating* the drug, than you ever do *doing* the drug. You may be at a house, and if the drug is not there, you're waiting for a big load to come in. Everybody's there at someone's house and the owner isn't even there! He's out getting drugs!

"But while they're out, the house is open and everybody is partying, or listening to somebody play guitar, zoned out, smoking pot until the meth connection gets there. People are filtering in and out. After you get tired of that scene you say, 'I know another place that probably has it'."

You go to another place and there might be the mother lode there. You might be busy for the next day or two getting rid of this great big amount of drug that you just paid your rent money for. You think you're going to make money on it, get your rent money back, but in the meantime you've used more than half of it yourself. You have nothing to sell at the end of it except maybe this small amount that you might be able to pay for the next amount of drugs with.

It's just a big, mad circle. Just goes round and round and round. At the time it makes sense. You don't see the truth of how crazy it is until you're totally out of that world.

But while you're in that dark world, you're addicted to a drug that creates hallucinations that can be scary and vile.

My mother-in-law had given me these little gnomes, the Seven Dwarfs, and I kept them on a shelf. Under the influence one day, I saw them talking to one another. I said to myself, *This is not real.* Then I'd look at that shelf again and they'd be laughing and cursing and saying just filthy, filthy things.

Because your mind is numb and you deal with so many other issues when you're up on meth for many days, you don't sleep. Your body is tired but your mind is just going like crazy. Meth isn't an hallucinogen but after so many nights of no REM (Rapid Eye Movement) sleep and watching filthy tapes, having so many filthy conversations, everything comes together and you see things.

Tabatha probably missed at least one day of school each week because I couldn't collect myself enough to get her out the door and on the bus.

I've heard so many women who tell about being on meth and seeing little worms in their faces, seeing worms in their car...

I had thought, *I will never be like those others on meth.*

But one morning I was getting my daughter ready for school and I was brushing her hair, fluffing it up, and I saw worms in her hair. They were like a computer generation. I knew it was an hallucination. I had to say to myself, *No, that's not what it is. That's not what it is. She doesn't have worms in her hair. You're on meth. That's not what it is.*

She got on the school bus and I worried about the worms in her hair. I cried and cried and cried, thinking, *I know that's not what it is.*

I tried to talk myself out of it. Pretty soon I wasn't thinking about it. I was thinking about a ton of other things. Picking at my face.

Meth chemicals are so caustic that when it comes through the skin, it causes the need to scratch and results in scabs all over your body. I picked at my face because I thought I saw blackheads. I was destroying my face with my fingernails.

Every day I would tell myself that I had enough will power to stay out of the bathroom, away from the mirrors. But each day I would, of course, need to go to the restroom and within seconds I would be so deep into picking at myself that I couldn't stop; picking at those blackheads I thought I saw in my face. I would lean into the mirror and pick at my skin until my entire face had pocks from my tireless obsession. Pretty soon I had my entire face picked and ripped to such a bloody mess again. Then I turned on my oven and stood close to the heating element so it would help clot my blood.

I never imagined myself so obsessed with destroying myself that I would put my daughter in front of the TV with "Barney" or "Blues Clues" for hours just so I could pick at myself. But I did. Every day.

All I could do was run from one room to the next, or stand in front of the mirror, or be stuck like a statue in the beams of sun so the scabs would dry. Then I'd pick at my arms or legs with such intensity that they would ache and itch from scabs.

I tried to sit with Tabatha to play a board game. I tried to pick so she wouldn't notice, as if she couldn't tell what I was doing. I would lay a towel across my legs while sitting crisscross in front of her. As she took her turn at the game I would lift the towel slightly, find a scab and begin to pull at my skin. By the end of our game I would have to go dress my wounds. My daughter would say, "boo-boo" and "doctor", and pat me on the back.

Surely my actions and my face were obvious to others, but it seemed that no one wanted to confront the issue.

When I was pregnant with Samantha, I was clean from all drugs. Chris and I were growing pot. We were living in a trailer and I'd sit on the floor with my legs criss-cross, and my fully pregnant belly "out to there", manicuring pot. Chris wasn't smoking pot at that point but he was doing meth and was really strung out much of the time he wasn't working. We grew pot to make money to buy meth.

After Samantha was born, I started smoking pot again and using meth. We'd take the girls to Chris' mom's house then after dark I'd drop him off at the pot patch with his water jugs.

One night I'd been up several days on meth and smoking pot. After dropping him at the patch, I stopped at an intersection a couple of miles down the road. I looked to my left where there was a long field. In the moonlight I saw police motorcycles lined up from one end of the field to the other. I heard the *baroom-baroom* of the cycles. They were bopping over the field toward me.

I panicked. I hit the accelerator and drove as fast as I could, knowing the cops were behind me on their motorcycles. It was a miracle I didn't crash. I lost my way and found myself across the state line. I was on the on-ramp and looked down at the speedometer. I was going only five miles an hour! Cars were all backed up behind me. I managed to pull over but I didn't know how to get back to the patch.

I crept into town. I didn't know where I was, though I'd been to this town many times over the years and was thoroughly familiar with it. I thought, *Okay, I can find my way back from here.*

But I couldn't. I stopped at a convenience store to ask directions. The clerk would tell me and I'd get back in my car and drive off the lot, and couldn't remember what he'd said. Then I'd find another convenience store and ask the same question, then another and another. Actually, I was getting farther and farther away from where I needed to be.

When I finally did find my way back across the state line I was an hour late picking up Chris. I thought, *He's going to be so mad at me.*

I drove by where I'd dropped him off, looking for the flash of the flashlight to let me know where to stop but didn't see it. So I drove on, circled the field and came back around, made sure no one saw me.

Finally I saw the flash and he came up. He said he was a little late so I admitted I was late, too. I told him what had happened and that I'd driven around the field two or three times. Then, of course, I was the bad guy; someone might have seen me. He had been up for days on meth so he was just as paranoid as I was. As we drove off, we were fully convinced that someone was hanging back, watching to see where we drove.

Along with hallucinations there's always that kind of paranoia.

One night, we were at a friend's house, who lived in a very remote spot. There was nothing out that far from town, so the Sheriff's patrol never patrolled the road, much less go down this driveway. But this night the squad car was patrolling this road…and pulled into and drove all the way down the private drive. There were trash bags of pot all over the living room, and they sort of freaked out, but the patrol car just turned and left.

Another time, Chris was out in the patch and saw a big van, right in the middle of a field. Chris didn't understand how the patrol couldn't have seen something, why they weren't discovered and arrested.

That night I didn't realize that seeing the motorcycle cops, hearing them, was a hallucination. I saw those motorcycle cops. I heard the sound of those cycles.

The hallucination and paranoia like we experienced are a part of drug usage. They are from Satan. I know demons are real. We who have been there know the perversions; the filthy things people say and do are demonic. But at the time they are a part of life. A part of the darkness that is the world of meth addiction.

> The hallucination and paranoia like we experienced are a part of drug usage.

So many people with a meth addiction aren't discovered, aren't arrested. I don't understand that. The problem is so obvious. The meth problem is enormous. I presently work for Early

Childhood and Special Education for a school district. They screen children to assess them to see if they qualify for the program. I'm not a certified teacher, but I'm a teacher's aid and part of my job is to keep the kids entertained during the assessments, by doing things at a table with them between tests.

The parents sit in the gym talking, waiting to go talk with the counselor about their child's assessment. The number of parents in which I see the signs of meth addiction, or are high on meth is amazing. The whole time they're sitting there they're squirming, picking at themselves, totally oblivious to the fact that anyone is aware of what's going on with them.

I've watched people in my home squirm in their chair, stand up and run their hands up and down their body, unable to sit still, just talking-talking-talking. I've been there myself. I remember that and think, *I* enjoyed *that?*

I'd look at my face in the bathroom mirror, picking at it, pulling the scabs off my face with shaking hands, not able to talk on the phone because my voice was so shaky. I couldn't write anything because my hand was trembling so I could hardly hold a pen. I knew what was going to happen before I put meth in my system but I *needed* it so badly.

The darkness was growing deeper and deeper but I didn't see any way out or even want out then.

Praise God I don't look like that any more. I have a few scars on my face, but considering what I did to my body it's not what it should be. They're not noticeable because God has been really, really gracious to me. I've lost a lot of teeth. Not in the front.

Again, that's His grace. But none of my molars are any good. The dental decay that is a part of the result of meth addiction is very evident to everybody. An addict's teeth are missing or blackened, chipping off, but most addicts just don't see it.

We don't see the trap; we don't see the enemy (Satan) until he devours our life, but there is hope. The beautiful thing is, when you come to the Lord, it doesn't matter what kind of ugly you've been splattered with. God restores. He gives you beauty for ashes. He's so gracious. Christ Jesus. Yes!

God restores. He gives you beauty for ashes. He's so gracious.

a great light

...the people dwelling in darkness have seen a great light, and for those dwelling in the region and shadow of death, on them a light has dawned.

Matthew 4:16 ESV

While pregnant with Samantha, our second child, I'd stopped smoking pot, stopped using meth, and Mini Thins. Stopped smoking cigarettes. I was completely clean from everything. I ate everything under the sun! I walked three miles every morning. I was going to be the perfect mother. Again. I'd laid it all down. Again.

There were some complications at her birth. She'd swallowed amniotic fluid so she was immediately rushed away and IVs put in so she wouldn't get sick from the fluid. She was given a bottle in the nursery so she had difficulty latching onto me, and I couldn't breast feed her. That was all the excuse I needed to begin using meth again.

At the time we had one vehicle so I'd take Chris to work. He was working the three-to-eleven shift. In order to get our drugs, he'd make the deal then I would drive to get an "eight ball". Then we'd decide whether we were going to sell part of it, make some money, or just do it all. It all came down to that last year—chaos.

Chris worked Sundays, and because of our one vehicle situation, I stopped taking the girls to church. But my neighbor came to offer a ride to church for as long as we needed it.

Since my whole life was based on illusion, I thought taking my kids to church helped hide the monster inside of me, help me look better.

"Sure. I'll see you around 10:45."

"We go to Sunday School," she said, "so I'll be here at 9:30."

Again, my illusion demanded that I be a good "church going" mommy.

"Sure. Sounds great!"

I went to a Sunday School class that was studying the book of Nehemiah verse by verse. Just like when I was in school, I needed to be the "best student", so I studied. Here I was, still with all my addictions, studying the Bible. I made sure all my homework was done so when we met the next Sunday I'd have my verses, my references, finished "perfectly".

As I studied, I read how God honored Nehemiah for going against the grain and listening to his heart. I read about the people who had sinned and rejected God's guidance and I began to think (*all the time*) about how awesome it would be if I could confess *my* sins to others and to God like it said the Israelites did at the gate of the city of Jerusalem. Just leave them all behind.

An eighteen-year-old young woman was very important to my life at this point. She was our landlord's daughter. We had lived in the house for about three years so we'd watched her grow up. She was so sold out to the Lord. So in love with Jesus. She'd earned the money to go on a mission trip to Russia. From time to time she would talk to me about little things. She didn't know I was doing meth, or that I had smoked a joint before I saw her.

We'd been late with rent so many times that I thought I had to offer my special little favors to my landlady to make me feel better so I was weeding her flower garden out front one day when her daughter came out to help me. She felt so good about serving God and was telling me something that God had put in her heart. She didn't know that the Holy Spirit was working in my heart at the time.

> She talked about the blessings of God, how good He was, and how she was so glad she was in love with the Lord.

"You know what's great about God?" she said. "No sin is on a greater-than or lesser-than scale than another sin."

I grabbed hold of that. *There's no greater-than or lesser-than scale when it comes to sin! What does that mean, no greater-than or lesser-than scale?*

I thought about that. Then I began to believe it was true. I knew I'd heard that in church. Sin is sin. Sin separates us from God. That's it! You just have to ask God to forgive you and He rids you of all blame. Because He can—because He's God!

Chris and I had friends at our house one night and we all smoked a joint on the back porch. I decided to let my husband and his friend know about this new-found understanding that I had about sin. The crazy thing is, sometimes when you're in the middle of doing your drug of choice you have these involved conversations about God. You're in this euphoric *thing*, you're contemplating the aspects of the universe, and you think you *understand* it all.

I told Chris and our friends what this young woman had said, that there's no greater-than or lesser-than scale when it comes to sin, when it comes to God looking at it.

"Then we're all sunk!" one man said.

"I know. I know that."

I remember thinking to myself, *That's true! We're all sunk. How in the world...*And I was just so...numb from that. I thought, *My goodness, we're all sunk. Every one of us. Every one who lives on the face of this earth!*

That's when God put in my heart that it doesn't matter how good or how bad you are. You just have to ask Him to forgive you...no more sinking ship.

It was very shortly after that that I asked the Lord into my heart.

I have often said that my daughter, Tabatha, is the reason that I gave my heart to Jesus. And in part, this is true. But I think to be fair, Samantha, who was almost twenty-two-months-old at the time, played an equal role.

I remember the day that I saw *me* through her eyes. I was washing dishes and she was talking to me (amazingly fluent for her age). As I carried on a conversation with her, I was smoking a cigarette in the corner of the kitchen. Samantha was sitting on the floor close to the cabinet. I had a fan on the counter to blow my smoke so that it was undetectable, except for the smell, of course. I never wanted my children, or any child for that matter, see me do anything that I as a child watched my parents do; something that they seemed to think more important than I was to them. It was painful to realize that their cigarettes and my dad's alcohol was more important than I was.

Every couple of minutes I leaned deep into the counter so my face was hidden, to take a drag and blow the smoke out before I went back to talking to her. She was small enough that I thought I could easily hide something as long as it was high up enough, out of reach and out of sight.

You see, I never *wanted* to be addicted to cigarettes, pot, speed, drugs of any kind. But I was trapped and now it was my responsibility to be a mom without showing my weaknesses. I felt I had a split personality at times. Many times I talked with other mothers that I partied with who were as scared as I was about the trap we were all in. Some of them had no idea that what they were doing was as ugly as it was, but most of them had the same feeling of living two separate lives that I had.

So this day, as I exhaled and then changed into my mommy personality, I turned and found myself face to face with Samantha who had stood up on tiptoes and was watching me. She had the most puzzled look on her face. As my expression changed into shock and fear, hers did, too.

As my expression changed into shock and fear, hers did, too.

All of the years of hiding, sneaking, and lying came flooding back. The problem was that I still blamed Chris for my addictions. Someone else had to be responsible, not *me!* When I tried to explain to him that I hated myself for what we were doing, he told me it was *my* problem. My anger increased.

At this point we had stopped doing meth (though we still did other drugs and alcohol) and Chris was furious.

"What else do you want to take from me?"

After screaming at each other continually, and our kids crying because the two people they were supposed to be able to trust couldn't be depended on for the smallest thing—their comfort—we split up. Again. We were still living the life my parents had lived; the life I had always hated.

Now that my husband no longer had to answer to me, he began using meth more heavily than before. After he was unavailable to talk for a day or two, Chris would then call non-stop for a couple of days.

Those of you who are or have been involved with the world of meth understand that this is typical behavior. You have been involved in fights where you or your loved one has gotten out of a vehicle and run away screaming at the other, or even perhaps jumped from the car while it was still moving.

Maybe one or both have destroyed precious mementos of the other in a selfish aim at making them feel as bad as you do inside. Most cases are born out of an inability to deal with the flood of emotions that surface on the "down side" of a high. Typically though, after a few years of using meth, it's just a way of life to act and react horribly with those people you once loved so much.

That's how it had become between Chris and me. We simply didn't know how to love each other, and by this point we really had no reason left to love each other.

Though I was not yet saved, I was talking to God all through my day and I was studying the Bible verse by verse, contemplating the thought of that "scale" of sin. I talked to God about my kids, about my husband as I walked the length, back and forth, of our trailer. I was bargaining with God.

"Oh God, if you'll just fix my marriage I'll really teach my kids about You, take them to church…"

The very minute I presented that final *bargain* to God I felt His presence and heard His voice touch every cell of my body. It was like a…thunder in my body. I *knew* God was talking to me. *No more bargaining,* was all He had to say and I was down on my knees on my dining room floor, sobbing and confessing and asking God to forgive me. Up to this point, I had thought of a *reason* for every sin that I practiced. I blamed my parents for not raising me in a stable home, my husband for *my* unfaithfulness to our vows, God for my child's disability, the car in front of me for making me late to work. On and on and on. But the truth was, I created the messes in my life with my own poor choices. The realization sent me to my knees.

But the truth was, I created the messes in my life with my own poor choices.

There on my knees before God I wept and wept and wept. I gave myself over to God. "I'm so sorry….I want to change…today."

I was SO sorry! I can't tell you how regretful I was. Suddenly I took responsibility for everything. God made me see the choices I'd made. All of that was ripped out of my heart. I was so sorry I made that choice. I was so sorry; *I need You to save me from myself. I need You in my life, God.*

I don't know how long I was on the floor but it was certainly long enough for me to dump all my baggage at the Lord's feet. He met me right there.

When I rose to my feet I'd never felt such peace in my life. I wasn't sure for a moment whether my feet were touching the ground. I breathed the sweet air of forgiveness. My weight was gone; my sins had been forgiven. He gave me such peace.

my healer

As for me, I said, O Lord, be gracious to me; heal me, for
I have sinned against you!

Psalms 41:4 ESV

I remember watching an old *Little House on the Prairie* episode
where the doctor had to reopen a huge wound in a man. The
pain for the patient was so horrible and everyone was question-
ing the doctor whether this was wise or not. But he said, "If
we don't do this then infection will take his life." That's exactly
what happened to me. I was infected with sin and it would have
taken my life without God's healing. Jesus Christ, the Great
Surgeon, opened me up so all the poison flowed out that day on
the floor of that little trailer. He's my healer.

I had to tell Jesus about my unfaithfulness, say out loud that
I did meth while trying to raise a special needs child who is a
gift from God, and Samantha who is an equally blessed gift. I
had to tell Him about my problem of always being concerned
about how people saw me; say that out loud. Like the doctor
dealing with the wounded patient, I had to be opened up in
order to be healed from the inside out. I had to trust God.

I had to trust God.

For so many years there were so many lies. I could never allow my separate worlds to come together because people might actually talk, learn the truth. But when I began saying aloud all the secret "stuff", it was like none of that mattered any more. I had dealt with so much pain for so long, trying to keep my different worlds apart, that I thought, *Even if it hurts a whole, whole lot then it can't be a prolonged pain.* I'd lived so long under this umbrella of oppression, because I'd tried to hide, tried to live secretly, that I just wanted to get it all out!

Jesus helped me. He didn't take the scab off Himself. He said, *You're going to have to remove it. I'm here to heal it when it's open, but opening it has got to be your move.*

The first thing I wanted to do after I got up off my knees was call my husband and tell him about all the things that I'd lied about for the twelve years we'd known each other. That day God had placed in my heart a secure knowledge that if everything was about Him, He was all about saving my marriage. I knew that whether or not my husband did his share to salvage our marriage, God was going to see me through anything. But regardless of the outcome I still had a million confessions from my lifetime of bottled up lies.

One of the first things I learned after being saved a while was that I had a responsibility for *walking* out my salvation. Not just *working* out my salvation, but *walking* out my salvation with the Lord. That God, that Jesus Christ, has a responsibility to me. Not that He must answer to me in any way, except that He made a solemn promise to me. *I will be responsible for your life, now you've got to make the first move by turning it over to me. I'll be your healer, but you've got to be willing to open up and be raw. When you do that you will heal the right way, the way I intended.*

For most of my life I really thought that if my heart was right I was okay. I had some knowledge about God. When my dad was drunk he talked about God. I'd learned some things in Sunday School as a child, when I went. But I thought, *Why would a good God, a just God, expect me to be perfect? I love my neighbor as myself.* I thought of my family, *My mother, brothers and sister would give anyone the shirt off their back and die freezing. How could a truly just God reject somebody that believes who He is?*

Well, He doesn't expect us to be perfect. Just forgiven, and willing to follow Him.

You've got to say, *I can't do eternity without You. I know I can't live the rest of my life, or live forever, without You. I'm a sinner. Please forgive me.* Then not only say it, but live it. Follow His ways, and not your own. Not only is it *not* hard to do, but it is so wonderful to release that responsibility of guiding your own life to now letting Jesus direct you.

I had to come to that point. It happened on the floor of my dining room that day when I gave my life to the Lord, even though I didn't understand everything. I knew my soul was eternal. Period. But was it going to be eternally in hell or eternally in the presence of the Lord? All these things came rushing in. I needed Him to forgive me! And He did.

I'm SO in love with my Lord. One of the super great things about my marriage right now is that I love my Lord more than I love my husband. Does that sound strange? But Chris' perspective is the same. God is our focus. All else is secondary. We both understand and believe that. How wonderful it is to me to see my husband praise the Lord without worrying about me at all.

I love my husband. He and my children were given to me by God Almighty. But it's not about Chris. I'm so in love with him but I have a Lord who has been my teacher, my healer, my savior, and I bow to Him every day because He deserves it.

A day without God would be the worst thing to live through. If He removed His blessing from my life, removed His hand from me today, I would be in agony. Because if He removed Himself from me for any length of time I would be empty. He is the one who fills me up. He is my Lord.

> If He removed His blessing from my life, removed His hand from me today, I would be in agony.

jesus freak

You hypocrite first take the log out of your own eye and
then you will see clearly to take the speck out of your
brother's eye.

Matthew 7:5 ESV

After I asked Jesus Christ to save me, I called Chris who first
was sincerely shocked that I was calling him, second that I was
going on and on about all the things I needed to ask him to
forgive me for.

"Stop! Stop!" he yelled. "I don't want to hear from you. You
sound like a Jesus freak. I don't want to hear it."

I begged him to come home, this time because that's what I
thought I had to do to win him to the Lord.

It was the hardest thing in the world for me, but finally he
moved back into the house. Though we lived together, we lived
different lives. I tried to explain to Chris over and over that I'd
asked the Lord into my heart. I carried my Bible around and
told him about Jesus.

"Can't you understand?"

He hated me for a while. Because I wanted no part of the
drug world any more, Chris made fun of me to his friends.

"She found God. She's kinda crazy right now."

At that time, as our friends watched what was going on, and heard Chris tell them that I was "out of the loop," I was labeled "the big bad witch." I was the one who hurt Chris. I was the one who might be a narc now because I knew too much.

There's a verse in Proverbs about a woman tearing down her house with her own hands. When I read that I thought, *Ah!* I wanted to make sure I didn't do that. That scripture really just came alive to me. I wanted to avoid the "tearing down" part, but didn't quite understand enough to be successful.

Chris and I fought about everything, but mostly about me going to church.

"Why are you going there? You're just going to church with a bunch of hypocrites."

I didn't say anything but I thought, *That's not me. I'm not going to be a hypocrite.*

At church I'd hear, "God wants you to love your husband because he's part of you."

Then I'd come home from church and fight with my husband because he was drinking or he'd do a line of meth after he came home from work. Tabatha would walk up to her daddy, and I'd try to usher her away because he was high. I was actually reliving my childhood: dad high and mom scooping us up and ushering us out. I didn't want to live that double life any more. At the same time I was still taking MetaboLife, an over the counter diet pill, thinking it was okay because it was "all natural." I was beginning to lose the joy of my salvation and my new life with Christ and again began blaming it on Chris.

Meanwhile, Chris was out a lot. He'd say he was on a service call (for work). When I'd question him about it he'd say, "It's my job." But I would see no difference in his paycheck. I knew he wasn't on a call. He was out getting meth.

He was a runner by this time, but I didn't know a lot about it until much later. He would go into a store, and in the back he could buy as many ephedrines as he wanted. He spent hundreds of dollars on ephedrines and Sudafed. Nobody wants to do that part of it. Most people would think cooking meth is the one thing you don't want to do. But when you're cooking meth, you usually stay hidden, meaning no one usually knows where you are. We knew a lot of people who cooked meth, but nobody wanted to go get the supplies because that's typically where the police were watching. So it was the runner, people like Chris, who were really in danger of getting caught. But Chris did it because the runners get a lot of free stuff or a really good deal from the dealers.

He remembers leaving the store once with enough raw material to send him to prison for a long time. He went to a bar then was afraid to leave because he thought the cops were right outside, waiting to bust him. Paranoia.

This was Chris' life. I had my own.

I wanted my marriage to be better and I knew God had the answers for what was wrong. I would leave the Bible open to Romans because that was the first full book I read after coming to the Lord. I would leave the Bible open thinking, *He's gonna look at it. He's gonna look at it.*

But here's another "God thing". After I went to my knees and asked the Lord into my heart, Romans was the first book that I read. And I understood every word, drank it up. I was saying, "Oh Lord, yes! I understand that! God, I see that! Oh, thank you, Lord Jesus, I love you." I would say these things as I read and would weep and weep. I would try to do my housework but kept coming back to the table where the Bible was open and I would read some more. Pretty soon I was sitting down and reading it and weeping, saying, "Yes Lord, I understand that," and just loving it, loving His word.

Just a year ago, five years after I gave my heart to Jesus, I joined a class at our church that was studying the book of Romans. The study broke down the book verse by verse, explaining what it means and how it applies to us, how it applies to the Christian, and what God is telling us in this scripture. It seemed *so* complicated! I thought, *I understood every word of this before; how in the world could I have understood every word of this when I read it as a new Christian?*

Well, that was the awakening of the Holy Spirit! The Spirit was confirming in me who I am now, who He is in me, not that I actually understood the Spirit's work in me then. I can look back and that's one of those stakes in the ground I can go back to and say, *Oh, yes…I remember when God did this thing. I remember when God gave me full understanding of the book of Romans that I don't even have now, because I needed that then. I needed all that confirmed in my heart that day when I was reading it.*

But we have to be careful that when the Holy Spirit enlightens us about something, we *walk* in it. Absorb it then act on it.

But we have to be careful that when the Holy Spirit enlightens us about something, we *walk* in it.

When I was in the drug world, I thought I had a lot of friends. They weren't the kind of friends who stuck in there and encouraged me, but at the time I didn't know that. After I was saved I was a "Jesus freak" and those friends wanted no part of that. I didn't want to be around my old friends because it was a dark world they lived in.

I've spent many years being superficial with people so I find myself falling into that way of dealing with people unless God stops me and allows me to face my fears. When I do develop a relationship now it's an awesome thing.

As a result of the huge change in my life, and after I was saved, I didn't have significant conversations for about a year!

It wasn't that I didn't say a word, but every conversation was pretty topical. I didn't want to get to know anybody because I didn't know how to get through the day without telling at *least* ten different people at *least* ten different lies. Because that's who I had always been. I had always had separate worlds, and separate relationships. I became who I said I was, not who I really was, because I was running from the truth all the time.

After I was saved I would open my mouth to tell a story or something and it would already be so laced with lies in my mind that I would have to shut my mouth and just nod my head. The other person had to keep the conversation going because I couldn't add anything to it. (I often look back now and thank God for the "keeper" He placed on my lips.)

I was so judgmental of my husband that it was like daggers flew from my mouth. One minute I would say, "Okay Lord, please help me save my marriage. I believe you're going to make something wonderful out of this." The next minute I would say to Chris, "You don't love us. How could you think you're a decent person when you're doing drugs and your children are watching you and…" I cut my husband up into teeny-tiny pieces, and pushed him into the ground with my words. It was hard for me to say anything without using cutting and demeaning words.

That's the kind of person I had been all my life. So, that first year I lived in a lot of silence. And prayed a lot.

Chris and I continued to fight a lot. One weekend I couldn't stay any longer and I went to stay the weekend at his mother's house. I went to her church and at the end of the message the pastor asked everybody to bow their head and for anyone needing prayer to raise their hand. Weeping, I raised my hand and said in myself, *Oh Lord, I don't want to do this any more.* The pastor said, "I will pray for you right now."

I knew he prayed for me. He didn't know my situation and I don't know how many other people raised their hand, but I knew that prayer was for me. At that point I decided that I wasn't going to live miserably any more. I was a child of God. It wasn't my husband's standard, not the church's standard, but God's standard by which I had to live.

I'd read the scripture 1 Corinthians 7:1–16, but particularly verse 15 that says, if a man wants to leave, let him go. Don't fight to keep him there. I thought about all the times I'd begged Chris to stay with me because I wanted our family to stay together. I thought, If he ever leaves again I'll let him go peaceably.

When I got home Chris was packing his things.

"I'm leaving."

I thought, *Wow.*

"Okay."

"Well," he said, "aren't you going to throw a big fit? Aren't you going to get Tabatha crying? Aren't you going to—"

"No, I'm going to let you go."

He left.

I thought, *I'm not going to hang on to him. I'll get a divorce.*

I decided I would be single for the rest of my life. However, Chris would move back in one more time after this…which led to a series of events that would change our lives forever.

The Bible says the more you're forgiven the more you are grateful for. I have much to be grateful for. God has been so good to me.

Right then I wanted to fall in love with His church again, to be excited about going to His house and be joyful about being His daughter again. My decision was to hold on and stand up for Christ; to keep running my race, after all, the prize is Christ.

> My decision was to hold on and stand up for Christ; to keep running my race, after all, the prize is Christ.

A couple of years later, after Chris and I became facilitators for the open group for the Living Free ministry at our local church, we found that most unsaved people had strong opinions about "church people". When they walked into the open group from the street or from the jail they would say, "I don't really need to go to church to sit with a bunch of hypocrites."

My response to them is the same one I gave to my husband when he used to say the same thing, before he became a Christian himself. It's not about the hypocrites. I would rather go to church with them than to go to Hell with them.

I can tell you that none of that is important to me. All I care about was my relationship with God, my place in my church, being faithful and whole, and pleasing to God—that's freedom. This is the place that you have to get immediately after your commitment to the Lord. You have to understand that if you put Him first, loving what He loves, then He will give you the heart to love everything and everyone the right way, with the right motives and that it is more than enough.

If that makes me a Jesus Freak, I'm okay with that.

"they" are not "you"

And do not fear those who kill the body but cannot kill the soul. Rather fear Him who can destroy both soul and body in hell.

Matthew 10:28 ESV

One of the things that finally "clicked" with me after I was saved was that my concern with how others feel about me, about my recovery, is irrelevant. Recovery has to be based on how I am doing with God. God is the foundation on which I build my recovery, build a new life for myself. My devotion time with my Father in Heaven is my line of encouragement or discipline. His standard is my plumb line, not the standard anyone else might set.

Does that mean that my mom's feelings don't matter? Or that how my husband feels is not my concern? The answer is simple. When I devote my energy, time, focus, and devotion to a perfect God (who wants to give me the desires of my heart) *my ability to have right relationships* is now served on a plate of compassion given to me to glorify His name. In layman's terms, that simply means that I have really great relationships now. Now that my heart is right, so are my motives.

For those who are struggling with letting your loved one go, with giving them to God, here's some meat for you. Please hear this with an open heart. We serve a beautiful God. He is strong, powerful beyond anything we can imagine. He is able to do with your loved one what you have been trying to work out for years. Each time you have tried to help, each time you've depleted your finances because you see something good in your loved one and want to *do something,* or you plain ole hate what their problem is doing to your life and you want to help them because it's spilling over into your personal space, please know you're not alone.

We must understand that a part of recovery must be based on a healthy sense of the fear of God. This means to respect His authority and know that He can be *trusted* with the outcome of *anything* in our lives, and in the lives of our loved ones. We continue to live in disobedience because we are selfish. If we truly love God, it's all about Him. Not us.

The most difficult thing about being an addict, or loving an addict, is letting go and letting God be Who He is supposed to be. Letting God do or allow to happen what needs to happen in their life. I've seen parents come to the open group with their children—children in their thirties or sometimes older—crying, their heart broken. They have given their children everything they can but their child is still addicted, still struggling. We tell them—Let them go. The child must suffer the consequences of his own choices or he'll never make the choice to leave the drug of his addiction.

Stop trying to fix everything. It must be *their* choice.

Let go. Let them suffer the whole consequence of their choices (painful but necessary).

Let God. Let God be all He can be in your life, in their life (if they'll allow Him).

This doesn't mean you stop loving them. It means you love them in a different way, in a whole way, in a less enabling but more God-like way.

> Let them find out who they are as God begins to give
> them clarity.

There's a wonderful series of books by Max Lucado about the Wemmicks. Wemmicks are little wooden people that Eli, the woodcarver, has made. In one book called *You Are Special*, this little character named Lucia doesn't care about what anybody thinks about her because she spends time with her maker (Eli).

In the story, the Wemmicks walk around with dots and stars stuck to them. The dots are put on those Wemmicks who don't quite measure up, the ones that are always stumbling and falling, the ones who have chipped paint and aren't so pretty.

"That's a poor Wemmick," they say.

They put dots on them because they don't measure up to the ones who can act or do wonderful tricks, have a lot of money or material things.

"That's a good one," they say, and put a star on that Wemmick.

This little guy, Puchinello, who wasn't created so very pretty (in the eyes of the other Wemmicks), walks around covered with dots.

"I want a star so bad."

He's thinking of all these stars and dots of the world, all the approval and disapproval of others, and he doesn't quite understand.

Then along comes Lucia. Lucia has *not even one* dot or star on her! People want to stick dots on her, but they fall off. Others say, "Well, that's really interesting. I think she deserves a star!" So they try to stick a star on her and *it* falls off!

Puchinello asks her, "How come the dots don't stick to you like they stick to me? I can't get them off. How do they just fall off you?" She said, "It's easy. I just spend time with Eli, my maker. The dots only stick if you want them to." Puchinello gets curious and he goes to see Eli. Eli says, "Oh, Puchinello, I've been waiting for you."

The more time Puchinello spent with Eli, and got to know him, he began to have this feeling of hope. As he walked out the door a dot fell from him. Looking good for someone else no longer mattered. It was Eli's opinion, his maker's opinion, that mattered.

After I was saved I was grasping for a personality. I'd always lived in a false world, a world fabricated in my mind, a world where I worried about how people saw me. I was concerned about "looking good", seeming to be someone I wasn't. As a result, I truly didn't know who I was.

Through the simple Wemmicks story I learned you don't need a star or a dot. Your personality is yours alone. It doesn't matter what anyone else thinks about you. It was so hard for me to understand that because I'd led a staged life for so long.

I began to understand that I don't have to try to make a conversation "go just right". Either they are going to accept me because of who I am, or they're not. As long as I am doing what God expects of me, I shouldn't worry about the response of man. Either way is okay because "they" are not "me".

God wants us to move beyond the ordinary.

We are to live beyond self. As a child of God we are extraordinary. Someone has said, "God don't make no junk." We sometimes embrace "junk", but that's not God's choice for us. We move from ordinary to extraordinary when we're centered on Christ. When you come to Him, from that day on you're not "ordinary". You can live ordinary, but that's *your* choice.

Is "self" at the center of your life? Is "stuff" at the center? Make the choice to have Christ at the center and move from the mundane to the magnificent. Choose every day to live beyond the ordinary.

Another wonderful thing I learned after I was saved is that God is not bound by time or circumstance or anything that we are bound to in this life. He is perfect and infinite. He knows where we came from and what's going to happen in the end and He knows all the stuff we're going to go through in the middle. He gives us choices to have victory or to fail, and His grace even in the failures.

We can never understand how God could do such a thing, act so graciously in our life. So many things He saved me from, so many consequences I should have had. It's purely grace.

———————— ✳ ————————

I was wrapping myself in God's love and I wanted Chris to come to God, too. But to him I was still the Jesus Freak. For my thirty-first birthday, Chris gave me a Woman's Devotional Bible, but he didn't know it was an actual Bible. He thought it would pacify me. He thought it was just a devotional book. When I saw it was a Bible *I* thought, He's coming around! But, of course, he wasn't.

One of the hardest things I ever did after being saved was to actually listen to my heart (and not my intellect) and follow it. I'd been saved for about nine months when we went to his mother's house and left the girls with her so Chris and I could go on a "date." Chris was at the very worst of his addictions and knew I wasn't going to go out drinking or anything like that.

> One of the hardest things I ever did after being saved
> was to actually listen to my heart (and not my intellect)
> and follow it.

"Let's go play pool," Chris said.

"I won't go into a bar," I said, "because I'm not going to destroy my testimony. So whatever we do, it can't be in a bar."

Oh, he got mad! Got *so* mad! But he finally agreed.

"We'll go to the bowling alley."

He wanted to be able to drink. I didn't want to go but I knew Christians went there just to bowl so I thought it would be all right.

Let's go to the bowling alley and stop fighting.

By the time we got to the parking lot of the bowling alley, my husband was in a *rage*. Meth does that to you. One minute you might be calm, but the next in a full rage. Chris just exploded, and God forgive me, I fed his rage.

"You're acting 'holier than thou'. You've got no right to tell me where I can go and play pool. We're going to go to a bar and—"

"Just drop me here," I said. "I'll find my own way back. The girls and I will go home and you can do your own thing."

At that point I was done!

I was *done* because I saw absolutely *no* desire in Chris to change.

"Just leave me here," I said.

"Fine, get out."

I got out. Then he got out.

"No, you can just have the truck. Take it. I'm done. I'm done with you."

And he started walking away.

I thought, *Good. I'm going to have the truck! I'll have the vehicle and you can go.*

So I walked around to get in the driver's side but he turned and jumped in the passenger side.

"You're not going anywhere without me!"

That's the way we had fought for seven years while on meth. It was, I'm going to do this, No I'm not, I'm going to do this, No I'm not. Jumping out of vehicles, running in and out of the house in a fury because we didn't know what to do. It's a trap you're in and you have so much rage you don't know how to deal with the issue and you fight like little children. *Give me my way!*

"Just take me home."

"Okay," I said, and started driving.

He determined to go another way then and started pulling on the steering wheel. Any time I agreed with him he got mad and he was going to have his own way again.

We were swerving all over the road, screaming at the top of our lungs at one another. He grabbed me and twisted my shirt and ripped it, pinched me, pushing and hitting me as I was driving. The truck was nearly out of control and I was scared to death.

I don't remember exactly how it happened that we stopped at a convenience store but I think it was because I promised him that I would stay in the truck while he went in to get a beer. He said I'd better not leave him or there'd be hell to pay. He got out and started into the convenience store…and I took off.

I had decided I wasn't going back, I wasn't going to have anything to do with that life any more. Whatever happened from that point fell on Chris' own head. I was done. Just done.

I was only about ten blocks from his mother's house so I drove there, just crying and crying.

"Where's Chris?" she asked.

"You know what? I'm just going to tell you everything."

Chris' mother had remarried and, surprisingly enough, her husband is a recovered addict who had been saved and released from his addictions. I wanted them both to hear the truth. I told them about the years I had abused meth and had lied about everything, and that Chris was on meth now. I told her I was tired of playing the game, and I was not going to cover up for him any more.

I wasn't afraid of what she was going to think about me, about all the lies, because I was covered now. Forgiven. I was a Christian and was done living that old life.

"You're going to know the truth, mom, and you can deal with it because I'm *done*."

Then her husband asked, "Are you still using?"

"Of course not!"

"I had to ask."

I cried myself to sleep and the next morning the girls and I went home.

Chris went to her house the next day.

"I don't know what's coming out of her mouth but she's crazy. You can't believe a word she says."

His mom didn't know whether to believe him or believe me. She was prone to believe me because everything she'd seen and suspected over the years began to make sense. One thing she did do was to start praying, like the many years of prayers prior to this, but with a little better understanding.

I would never tell anyone that divorce is an option. I believe that God can save any situation, and restore any relationship. I also know that this point in my life and Chris' was our turning point. I had vowed to stop lying once and for all to everyone, and this left no more room for Satan to dig his claws into me. I had the right motives in mind when I stopped the cycle. My motives were to live right before my Lord, and my children. I didn't want my children to experience the same feelings that I had experienced of not trusting my mother for my safety. I was exhausted with trying to control Chris. I knew it was God's job to get Chris' attention, and knew that I was standing in the way as if I was telling God, "I've got it…no need for you to worry about Chris."

I believe that God can save any situation, and restore any relationship.

If this sounds like what you want to avoid, please take it from someone that has experienced the rat race cycle of codependency, and listen to God—just don't go there. Give your loved one to God in the very beginning. It will save a lot of heartache and energy. Praise God.

the beginning of transformation

For the grace of God has appeared, bringing salvation for all people, training us to renounce ungodliness and worldly passions, and to live self-controlled, upright, and godly lives in the present age.

Titus 2:11–12 ESV

The day following the crazy driving incident Chris kept calling me, threatening to come to the house, so I called the police. He did come and I was scared to death of him. He had been gone all night so I knew he had chemicals or something in his possession. When I told him the police were on their way he left again.

Chris called while the police were at the house and one officer wanted to talk to him.

"Sure, I'll talk to the police."

They talked for a few minutes and the officer told Chris that they would have to meet somewhere besides the house.

"Let's meet down by the river."

The officer told me he was going to arrest Chris so I needed to come so I could drive Chris' vehicle back home if I wanted it, so I went with him. They told Chris they were going to arrest him.

"Okay, so arrest me. But you've got nothing to charge me with."

He put cuffs on Chris and put him in the back seat of the patrol car. The officer told me to go home in the vehicle that Chris had been driving. I knew drugs were probably in that car and I didn't want to get stopped with drugs or other evidence in it so I refused to get in until the officer searched it.

I look back now and see that, deep down, I wanted to have Chris in jail for much more than twenty-four hours.

The officer searched the Jimmy. I thought he hadn't performed the search that needed to be done. I felt I could find what I knew had to be there because I'd been in the drug scene for so many years.

"If you don't mind I'd like to search and you can be my witness. I'm not taking this vehicle without a more *thorough* search because I know what's in it."

The officer agreed to watch me search.

I crawled all through that Jimmy looking for any kind of drug evidence. A straw, a razor blade, anything I could find. I went all the way through the front and back of that vehicle and found *nothing*.

I drove the Jimmy back to the house and the next day took out a restraining order against him.

Later on, after he'd given his heart to the Lord, he was remembering that day and told me, "You want to know something really crazy about that day? That police officer searched all the way through the vehicle and so did you, and didn't find a thing so there was nothing to charge me with. When the officer started searching the truck, I thought, *It's over.* In my truck was a coffee filter with meth in it. There was also pot, but he didn't find anything. When I got into the truck after I was released, there it was. Old bags, straws, chemicals. All of it. In plain sight."

God's wonderful grace and mercy. He blinded the eyes of the police officer, blinded my eyes. I'll never understand why. Chris could have gone to prison for a long time. He could have been sent away and not been able to have the experience of walking down to the altar and giving his heart to the Lord just a couple of months later.

Somebody who is living with meth today thinks they are living in hell. But I can guarantee that when they walk away and then look back and see time after time after time when they could have been dead, when they could have been arrested and sent to prison for the rest of their life, it's a different picture. Even those who landed in prison can recount the times they should have been dead but they weren't dead of an overdose because God had spared them.

We hear this all the time in the group sessions we facilitate. "I should have been dead because I should have overdosed on this amount, I should have…"

I look back on my own life and know that taking a hundred Mini Thins, 2500 *mg in one day,* should have killed me. I should be dead! Should have had a heart attack at taking ten! Only by God's grace I wasn't.

People live in unforgiveness, confusion, anger, when all they have to do is accept that the burden doesn't need to belong to them, but to God. Many psychiatrists will tell a person to hit a pillow if they're angry. All that does is feed the anger. God says that sin is crouching at your door and you must master it. The bottom line is that we cannot do life alone, and God will help us heal from the inside out. Dealing with anger or fear or hurt is His responsibility when we belong to Him. We just have to stay close to Him and do what He would do. When you surrender to Jesus, He lets you rest, then He helps you deal with the issues and learn the right way to search for them. Only God can tell you when it's time to do that. When you are stronger in Him you begin to see things with *His* eyes, not your own. When you put your eyes on Him and off of your situation, that's when the healing begins.

> People live in unforgiveness, confusion, anger, when all they have to do is accept that the burden doesn't need to belong to them, but to God.

Anybody who does *not* have a relationship with the Lord, a sold out, head-over-heels-relationship with the Lord, has a hole in their life. There will always be the desire to fill that void; something to fill that hole. Filling that emptiness with a drug, or alcohol, or even material things, or relationships doesn't satisfy and you're drawn deeper and deeper into Satan's trap.

The world tells us it's okay to do certain things. Television commercials, billboards, etc., tell you that to drink a beer is going to make you attractive to the opposite sex, that it's okay to trash talk.

In Ephesians 5:1–7 God tells us that's not the way we're supposed to act.

> Therefore be imitators of God, as beloved children. And walk in love, as Christ loved us and gave himself up for us, a fragrant offering and sacrifice to God. But sexual immorality and all impurity or covetousness must not

even be named among you, as is proper among saints. Let there be no filthiness nor foolish talk nor crude joking, which are out of place, but instead let there be thanksgiving. For you may be sure of this, that everyone who is sexually immoral or impure, or who is covetous (that is, an idolater), has no inheritance in the kingdom of Christ and God. Let no one deceive you with empty words, for because of these things the wrath of God comes upon the sons of disobedience. Therefore do not associate with them;

Ephesians 5:1–7 ESV

As Christians we're consecrated, devoted to God. That empty feeling inside can be filled only by God. Real, lasting satisfaction is found only by walking with Him.

That empty feeling inside can be filled only by God.

Sometimes I think I'm blessed that I failed miserably on my own. I needed a beautiful, wonderful, gracious God to pick me up and dust me off and walk with me. There are many people who are savvy businessmen and women who are financially independent, who are successful by the world's standard, but they have a void they're trying to fill. By the world's standards they're okay. Like the Wemmicks in the Max Lucado book. It's harder for them to come to grips with their need, to say they need the Lord, than it is for somebody like me. Yet if they are to examine their lives, they would find that there is a hole just as big as mine was…mine was just more evident.

Thank You, God, that I will always need you. Thank you for changing me, for the peace that you've brought into my life.

salvation

I will restore to you the years that the swarming locust
has eaten.

Joel 2:25a ESV

The night of horror that led to the morning of Chris going
to jail and a restraining order against him that lasted about a
month, resulted in Chris finding his own house to rent. All this
was a part of his road to salvation.

Chris hated being separated from his children. When we
were together, living for the enemy (Satan), he couldn't face
them because his shame was too great; but not being able to see
them at all was ripping out his heart.

That last year, before we separated, Chris had a routine, a
daily routine, of consuming as much alcohol as he could before
getting home, smoking a joint after he got home, and then would
sit in front of the stereo and listen to the song "Unforgiven".
He felt that what he had done in his life was too dark to be
forgiven.

> He felt that what he had done in his life was too dark to
> be forgiven.

When we separated the final time, he did as many drugs and drank as much as he could to try to fill the void inside him. Missing his children was so painful. He was not in love with *me* any more, but couldn't let go of the girls. (Thank God!)

As this God-Directed series of events goes, Chris went to the church which we now attend, led by his broken heart. He grew up in church, and felt that if there was any hope, it would be found with God. He went to church on the night our pastor says is the "most important service of the week", the Wednesday night prayer meeting.

Chris looked for someone to lead him to a group that was advertised on the sign outside as the Divorce Recovery group, but learned that another group wouldn't begin for a few weeks. The current group of people were in the middle of a series of lessons that built upon one another so joining in the middle would not be as beneficial.

Well, that was enough for him! He was on the way out of the door when someone stopped him. That man was sent by God to love my husband with Christ's love, the kind of love he had never experienced.

Even though Chris had alcohol on his breath and smelled like an ashtray, Mark hugged Chris and told him how brave he was to come and how much God loved him just the way he was. He invited him to go into the service…and Chris did. Mark practiced what Jesus tells us to do. Love one another with the love that He has loved us with, even when it's hard. Chris started attending church, because, as he put it, it was the only place he felt safe.

Over the next several Sundays pastor John preached from the book of Acts (no coincidence, but God's plan) about Saul's conversion. About how the worst sinner is still precious to the Lord, about surrender, and finally about the peace that comes with forgiveness. Romans 5:8 says, "But God shows us His love for us in that while we were still sinners, Christ died for us."

Chris thought he was too "bad" to be forgiven. This is exactly what the enemy (Satan) tells us. Satan pulls us into the pit of sin slowly, then one day we look at our lives and think we have done too much for God to forgive us. This is a lie!

God is, and has always been, waiting for you to ask Him to forgive you. At that moment it is *done!* Wiped clean! Forgiven! Forgotten!

> God is, and has always been, waiting for you to ask Him to forgive you.

So here it was. November 11, 2001…the day Chris gave his life to the Lord Jesus.

He walked the aisle, finally submitting to God. Every vein in his face stood out, the veins in his neck were bulging. He was crying so hard tears were flowing down his face.

Surrendering his will and his life to Christ was the first step that started a flame of commitment that is now a raging fire.

When I saw him after church he looked like ten years had been restored to his face. A peace had washed over him like I had never seen before. He still weighed only a hundred thirty-five pounds but he looked beautiful and innocent.

Since that moment so many things have happened that have moved us forward—not backward, not standing still. Chris is changing daily. His love for the Lord is growing.

But for a while after he was saved, he was still battling addiction. He was still using meth. He hated what he was doing but he didn't know how to stop.

We began going to the recovery ministry at church. I praise God for giving us a healthy church to grow in, a strong group of people who weren't afraid to help us deal with our issues and pastors who say what God wants His people to hear—truth.

I never wanted anyone to know that I wasn't the perfect mother. I wanted to keep that facade I'd created, especially with having a child with disabilities. Yes, I gave my child "therapy", but an hour a day, or even two, did not a mommy make. The children of addicts suffer.

After I walked away from using meth and I saw moms come into Living Free group sessions who had lost their children, I had the attitude of, *At least I never lost my children.*

I hate that I even thought that, because I should have had my child taken away. When I started using drugs again after I had Samantha, she should have been taken away, too. That was the worst of my abuse.

Meth makes you believe you're not hurting anybody but yourself. I always said, "I always have milk in the fridge for my kids. My kids always have milk." Or I said, "I always make sure my kids have food in front of them three times a day." But I might have fed them hot dogs four days a week, or fed them frozen fish sticks that you heat in the oven that many days a week.

Meals might have had the four basic food groups but it was something I could make in five minutes because I couldn't stand to be around food myself. I didn't want to eat and I didn't want to take the time to cook it.

I took care of Samantha. She had a bottle in her mouth, but she was with me when I went to pick up drugs. She was in the house when people came over. She was in the house when I smoked or did a line in the other room. She should have been taken away from me.

I don't know why she wasn't. Why Tabatha wasn't. That they weren't doesn't make me any better than anyone else. I was just a lot more fortunate.

It was Grace. God's grace.

A couple of weeks after Chris was saved I still said, "I'm not going back. What if he fails? I'm not going to be trapped in that."

I saw a difference in him but I was afraid to trust again. I'd watched my mom leave my dad, take him back, kick him out, take him back, again and again. Every time it seemed he had a true remorse for what he'd done. He would just *cry*. You could tell he loved us. But every time he came back we were again in the whirlwind of drugs, alcohol, abuse and everything that went with addictions.

So I told myself I wouldn't do that. I would *not* make that mistake again. *I've set a goal and I'm going toward it.* I'd already promised the Lord that I wouldn't have another man in my life because I knew Chris was the man I was supposed to have. *I love him but that's it. If he's walking with You, Lord, then at least the girls will have a good Christian home to go to when they go to their father's house.* That was just my mindset at the time.

I had agreed to let Chris have the girls for Thanksgiving weekend. *Oh, this is what it's going to be like. Split holidays and all the awful stuff that kids of divorced parents have to deal with.* I walked up to the door of the apartment he was renting in this "dump of a place" that was actually only one half of an old house where the upstairs had been made into an apartment, with another on the lower floor. When he opened the door the only thing missing was an apron around his waist.

He had candles lit, everything was clean, I could smell dinner cooking in the kitchen. I saw he was taking every precaution to make sure his girls were going to say, "Oh daddy, what a wonderful place and what a wonderful time we're going to have."

"Thank you so much for letting me have them."

He was hugging and loving on them and I just stood there and watched. It really hurt and I wanted to leave, but at that moment, God did a miracle in my heart and in the heart of my husband. I no longer felt the attachment to the unforgiveness that had settled in my heart. I knew that it was just like the day that I had surrendered to the Lord and He forgave me; there is nothing like it. It's not just peace; forgiveness is freedom. God just freed me from yet another chain. Chris felt it too. We understood that God not only forgave us for our individual sins, but He made it perfectly clear to us that He had forgiven the sins we brought into our union as man and wife. In our marriage vows we said that we swore under God to honor and keep one another, and we had done everything *but* that in the years we had been married. At this moment, however, the Holy Spirit wrapped His arms around us and took the pain of the memories away.

It's not just peace; forgiveness is freedom.

I was thinking, *What is going on...can I really believe this...*
I kind of backed toward the door.
"You could sit down for a minute if you want."
He sounded so grown up! He'd sounded like a child for so many years, and so had I. I'm not leaving myself out of it. We'd been such spoiled children for so long.
"Okay."
I sat down and listened to him talk with the girls.
"Do you want a drink? I've got some tea made..."
He was so polite and so excited that I would stay.
Pretty soon I was telling him about what the girls had done that week and the conversation started to flow. I was sitting on the couch with all of them and I started crying.
"What'd I say! What's the matter?"
"I can't leave."
Chris started crying. I didn't leave. I decided I could never leave.
All that fear that I had was very close, but it wasn't *in* me. It was hovering over my head ready to stick its claws into me, but I also knew that what I saw in Chris was real. It wasn't only that I saw he was sorry for what he'd done or even that he loved me and the girls. I saw a changed heart, something solid, and something peaceful; a peaceful look about him that I had never seen before.
When Chris went to the altar something happened in him that should happen to all of us. It takes more time for most of

us than it did for my husband, but God knew that Chris needed a new heart of forgiveness for himself and for others. He was no longer bound by the unforgiveness he once had for me or anybody else.

After I was saved I had the peace of salvation, but God had restored to Chris and to me a wholeness in this life that was stacked on top of that peace of salvation, an added blessing. It was…exhale, for a while.

God had placed in our hearts that day that as long as we looked to Him for our peace—not to each other—that He would handle the issues. That meant taking our eyes off of the circumstances, looking to Him, being obedient in the way we treated one another and other people, and He would give us His strength to accomplish what we could not. Praise God it's been more than five years since that day and it's gotten better and better. It's gone beyond grabbing hold of that peace. We have joy. We laugh out loud all the time. We are the goofiest family I know.

> God had placed in our hearts that day that as long as we
> looked to Him for our peace—not to each other—that
> He would handle the issues.

God touched us and gave us new eyes with which to see each other. We read His word every day and it spoke to us personally. Every sermon we heard was *about us*. The Holy Spirit was cleansing us.

I read *The Power of a Praying Wife* and Chris read *The Power of a Praying Husband*. We applied God's word to our situations. The rest of our "walking with the Lord" has been a process but the love that He gave us for each other that day was instantaneous. It is not only possible to save your marriage, but it is a promise, when both parties are fully devoted to God. I know that Chris is not always going to be perfectly in line with what I need, but if he is loving God more than he loves me, I can be sure that his motives won't be wrong, and his desires for our relationship will be right. In turn, Chris knows the same thing about me. Our love for God makes us love each other more purely. It's a powerful thing. God Power!

Our love for God makes us love each other more purely.

the will of sin

For if we go on sinning deliberately after receiving the knowledge of the truth, there no longer remains a sacrifice for sins.

Hebrews 10:26 ESV

We were in church one Sunday when our pastor, who never walks gingerly around any point when it comes to the Word of God, said something that brought about a huge change in Chris. Pastor John is going to tell you what the Word says, then it's the Holy Spirit's job to deal with how God applies it to your heart.

Pastor said something to the effect of, "If you are in the middle of a sin and you are *continually* sinning the same sin and you know that blatantly you're doing it and it disagrees with the Word of God, you've got to start wondering where you stand. You understand by the Holy Spirit's prompting that it's a sin— more than likely people start doubting your salvation. It's not our place but by your fruits you are known. You've got to start talking to God and asking, Am I really saved?"

Whatever else he said, that's all my husband heard. Chris was saved and he loved God with all his heart, but he was still using meth and that sermon made him furious. When I looked at him I saw anger and hurt begin to well up inside him. I believe that one way you reject the Holy Spirit is with continual blatant sinning. Pretty soon your heart becomes hard to the truth. I believe it was right at that point in my husband's life that the Holy Spirit was saying, *Listen to this. You're either going to become completely hardened soon or you're going to listen to this. This is me prompting you again.*

> I believe that one way you reject the Holy Spirit is with continual blatant sinning.

As soon as church was dismissed, Chris said, "I'm leaving." He headed back up the aisle and Mark, the man who led Chris to the Lord, was walking across that side of the sanctuary. Our church is very large and Mark doesn't usually sit on our side of the sanctuary. But he was right at the top of the aisle Chris was striding up with me following. I looked at him, crying, "He's going to leave!"

Mark said, "No, he's not. You get the girls, I'll get Chris."

Mark went after my husband and all I could do was just trust that whatever was going to happen was going to happen for the good. Again I had to totally give it to God right then. *Lord, if he's going to leave me, if I'm going to be left with no husband, You're my husband from here on out. I cannot dwell on, Oh no, what if I lose him? Oh no, what if I don't have his income? What if I don't have his warm body to hold me? What if I don't…I can't be afraid of that any more.*

I camped on that prayer for the fifteen to twenty minutes that I sat in my Sunday School class while Mark talked to Chris. Finally he came to get me.

"Get your purse and come on."

I told my class table leaders that something was very wrong and we needed prayer, and they began praying for us.

Mark took me to a small chapel and Chris was there along with Mark, his wife Shelli, and a handful of leaders in our church who were not afraid to pray the prayer that needed to be prayed.

They all gathered around and Mark said to Chris, "I'm not letting go of you. God's not going to let go. You're my brother. We're going to ask God to deliver you. Okay?"

I was crying, Chris was crying, our girls were plunking on the keys of a piano in the corner. Everyone was praying aloud and I don't remember if the girls had stopped playing the piano or if it was just that the prayers being offered up to God from these wonderful people brought the quiet, but there was a hush that came over everything. These people prayed an honest prayer that God would deliver my husband, that He would stop the enemy from taking my husband away, that He would give me courage. I was encouraged to rest in God, to step back and let God do what He needed to do. It was amazing.

We didn't talk most of the way home. Finally Chris said, "I need to thank you."

I said, "I thought you were going to hate me forever."

He said, "I hate this…not you."

He wasn't sure what he'd say to the man who offered him meth. Every day he saw him, this man would offer him a line. That's the way our meth usage and addiction had started and the way Chris' had continued. Chris didn't know how he'd say no to this man, but his opportunity was soon given.

The next day Chris found that his "connection" had been moved to another area.

When we trust Him, God is going to move a mountain.

Unfortunately, Chris was still under the assumption that God was going to take the "craving" for the drug from him so he wouldn't have to struggle with decisions. Not so! He still used, but now he was looking for meth and wondering why God wasn't "helping" him in his endeavor to give it up.

One very distinct attribute of God is that He cannot counsel against Himself. In other words, God will never go against what He has already laid as a foundation for having a relationship with Him. He gave us "free will" from the very foundation of the earth. He tells us that He will never force us to love Him. The Bible tells us this:

See, I am setting before you today a blessing and a curse: the blessing, if you obey the commandments of the Lord your God, which I command you today, and the curse, if you do not obey the commandments of the Lord your God, but turn aside from the way that I am commanding you today, to go after other gods that you have not known.

(Deuteronomy 11:26–28 ESV)

God wanted Chris to realize that it was his choice to say "No" (free will) and God's pleasure to say, "Good choice, my son. Now comes My strength; now comes life."

> Chris finally surrendered it all to a Holy God and gave up meth.

The next time Chris spoke with his connection, everything was different.

"Guess you don't want any of this."

"No," Chris said, "I don't."

Oh, how good God is to give us His Holy Spirit. As Chris began standing on God's word, he believed the Lord when it said that he would never be given more than he could handle, and always give him a way out. That if he thought about good things, pure things, and not the things that would pull him back, that God would give him the strength to say no to ungodliness. God says that because we love Him,…He will rescue us, and deliver us, and protect us. So Chris began to pray these scriptures. Meaning he had an ongoing conversation with the Creator of the universe…all day long. He knew that if He was in the Lord's presence, that he was safe. Nothing was impossible.

Walking away from meth was one of the hardest things Chris has ever done, but when he said "no" it was over. God was there. Meth was still available every day, but it didn't matter. He wasn't drawn to it any more, didn't struggle with it every day. He was *delivered.*

Nothing is too hard for God. Chris thought that the addiction was bigger than anything, that he couldn't give it up. But it wasn't just that he was delivered. It was confirmed in his heart by God—*The day you were saved was the day I delivered you. The choices you made in between were your choices, but I gave you that deliverance on that day. When you asked for it, I gave it to you.*

Nothing is too hard for God.

I've heard it said that when somebody gives you a gift, you don't just look at the paper and say, "What a pretty bow!" and set it aside. You open the gift. You enjoy the gift.

God gives us gift after gift through our lives. Receive what He's given you. Open it. Enjoy it.

Another "God thing" is that when Chris quit meth, just like when I quit, there were *no* withdrawal symptoms and *no* repercussions from the people he'd run for and used with. God took care of that. He is amazing. His work in our lives is perfect love, grace, and mercy.

The people Chris knew before, when we were in the meth world, weren't his friends any more. There had never been a real *friendship*. They said, "Well, he's not doing meth any more so…" Those who are running with others who do meth are always so concerned about someone thinking they have "turned narc" if they quit. The truth is no one really cares! If you are out of the scene, stay out, and trust me, sooner than you would expect, you are no longer relevant to them. They are very soon thinking about a multitude of other things, not you.

In the meth world, everyone thought everyone else was calling the cops. It was so twisted. Everyone was paranoid. You can't hang out with the same people after you quit. We have nothing to talk to these people about.

"I don't want to hear about the bad deal going down or whatever," Chris said. "We have real friends now."

We thought we knew what having friends meant. But as we sat in church a few months ago and I looked around—the people we know sort of congregate in one area—I was blown away. These are true friends. They aren't friendships based on what you can do for me as before, with the "meth people".

Now our life is about what *I* can do for *you*. A Christ-like love exhibited in each one, and in us. This was the kind of love that God had placed in our hearts, but we needed an example to walk us through the process. We prayed for "Kingdom Friends." Again, God was faithful. He sent to us precious friends who when we looked at their lives, we saw real living *in* this world, but not *of* this world kind of people. Kevin and Candra and their family allowed us to invade their lives with the "raw" issues that we faced every day. We didn't know how to trust people; they taught us how to let go of the fear. We didn't know how to meet new people; they had us over for every party they had, and showed us how easy it was to have fun meeting new friends. But mostly, they taught us how to love the Lord with our lives; how to trust Him when everything was falling down around us. They showed us that it was okay to cry and laugh all at the same time; I'm so glad that God sent them to us. He will do the same for you, all you have to do is ask.

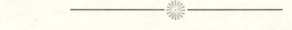

One of my favorite things is getting "caught" praying by my oldest child. Tabby sometimes wakes and comes into my quiet place while I'm praying. At one time I prayed silently for fear of waking my girls. Not that they would be afraid, but I thought it would shorten the time I spend with the Lord.

My dear friend, Shelli, just laughed when I told her why I prayed so quietly. She gently told me, "Oh Debra, what an awesome way for your girls to wake up! What a testimony that is to them!"

She was right. What an awesome thing it is. So now when I pray I don't dampen the loud cries that sometimes come out as I talk to my Father. When Tabby hears and comes in, she quietly sits crisscross before me, gently takes my hands and agrees with me in prayer that we serve a wonderful God.

What an awesome way for my child to wake up. My joy overflows, again and again.

One Sunday morning we were getting ready for church and I watched both our girls dance before their father. They each had on a pretty dress and as Samantha began to twirl she said, "Look, daddy, see how it twirls so beautiful?" I then saw our oldest join in to win the affection of their daddy as well. Together, twirling and giggling. I ran to our bathroom and dropped to the floor, praying to my Father that that memory would stay forever.

Our children adore their father and it's quite evident that I have nothing to do with fostering that relationship. They built it on their own. I didn't do *anything* to receive these wonderful blessings. The only thing I did was surrender one day, on the floor of that little trailer, to an Almighty God who had been calling my name for a long time.

> Our children adore their father and it's quite evident that I have nothing to do with fostering that relationship.

I tell my story not to elevate myself in any way but in the hope that it might help someone understand that through all of the "mess" of my life, character was built in me. Not in the past, but after I surrendered my heart to the Lord. The Bible tells us that God gives us beauty for ashes, strength for tears. This is love.

to grant to those who mourn in Zion—
to give them a beautiful headdress instead of ashes,
the oil of gladness instead of mourning,
the garment of praise instead of a faint spirit;
that they may be called oaks of righteousness,
the planting of the LORD, that He may be glorified.

Isaiah 61:3 ESV

A crown instead of ashes put on the head as a sign of mourning. A transformation from sorrow to joy and praise. A spirit of burden released to one of praise and gratitude for what God can and will do in your life.

Just ask. He's waiting for you.

consequences

I can do all things through Him who strengthens me.

Phillipians 4:13 ESV

Consequences. For every action there is a reaction. There are always consequences to our actions, to the choices we make. None of us lives in a vacuum, so our choices affect someone or something else in our lives. Even after we're saved we bear the responsibility for those choices.

Two years after I was saved, my husband and I were to be part of an interview for a program to be televised locally called *Isn't It Amazing,* a Christmas program presented by our church choir. Our part of the program was about our addictions and deliverance. I was nervous about doing it.

A couple of days before the interview I was in the workout room at my work and I thought talking through what I would say would make me more comfortable. I began telling my story to this one woman and pretty soon I was the only one in the room talking! The other woman, well, her mouth had just dropped open in disbelief.

"I probably should have let you know that my husband wasn't the only bad guy. You guys know I was delivered from drugs."

"I thought you did drugs before you had your first child, not after."

"No, I started doing meth after I had Tabatha."

"How could you ever do that? How could you ever start doing drugs after God gave you such a special gift of that child?"

She was so serious and she looked at me with such disgust.

"I know it's not my place to judge," she said, "but I can't understand why you would do such a thing!"

This was the first time that someone had put me down instead of saying, "Oh dear, thank you Lord that You delivered her." It was the first time that somebody told me, "Shame on you."

> It was the first time that somebody told me, "Shame on you."

I didn't know how to react. I was suddenly afraid to do the interview because I might face rejection. What if all of Tabatha's teachers, her principal, people I dealt with in the Individual Education Program meetings for Tabatha found out? Chris had quit using just a few months before our interview. His dealer might be watching the program. How could Chris stand up in front of many, many people across this area and say, "I was delivered from meth."

I said, *God, if you're asking me to do this for You, You're going to have to give me the courage to stand in front of people and say, Yep, I did something very wrong but I'm not that person any more. I'm a*

brand new creation. All of that happened, but I'm done with it. I'm
not going to wallow in it any more.

Every time we go back and pick up our fear of man's opinion, it creates a hook that holds us in the world. It keeps us out of God's perfect will, out of His freedom.

> I tell you, my friends, do not fear those who kill the body,
> and after that have nothing more that they can do. But
> I will warn you Whom to fear: fear Him who, after He
> has killed, has authority to cast into Hell. Yes, I tell you,
> fear Him!
>
> Luke 12:4–5 ESV

When some come to God they think, *He's going to throw me into hell if I don't walk a straight line.* The old fire and brimstone preachers give us that idea of who God is. Live for the Lord! Or die in a burning lake of fire!

That's not how God wants us to see Him. It's Satan who draws us into death and hell. It's God who offers salvation and life. All through scripture He says, Come to me, learn from me, you'll find rest in me, you'll find hope in me.

We must understand God's attitude toward sin. He hates it; we must hate it. That's why we never crack open the door and look at temptation because we must hate sin as much as He does. The temptation is not a sin. It's the decision to give *in* to temptation, that's the sin. If we never look at what tempts us, then we're not going to give in to it.

> Let no one say when he is tempted, I am being tempted
> by God, for God cannot be tempted with evil, and He
> himself tempts no one. But each person is tempted when
> he is lured and enticed by his own desire. Then desire

when it has conceived gives birth to sin, and sin when it
is fully grown brings forth death.

James 1:13–15 ESV

The evil is in us. When we are trapped and enticed, it is by our own evil desires. Lust (a desire for anything not of God) becomes sin and the consequences of sin is death. Our society says it's okay to be a little raunchy, a little sinful. My husband and I gave up watching television nearly four years ago, except for some PBS programs, because too many shows present the idea that it's okay to be sexually immoral in some way, to be gay, to be promiscuous, to practice fornication, adultery. All of these things are glorified in our society. Chris and I refuse to open the door to even the idea of temptation. And we don't take lightly the things we allow into the heart and mind of our beautiful children.

Do not love the world or the things in the world. If anyone loves the world, the love of the Father is not in him.
For all that is in the world—the desires of the flesh and
the desires of the eyes and pride in possessions—is not
from the Father but is from the world.

1 John 2:15–16

Lust wants to get. Love wants to give. Lust looks at people as objects. Men involved pornography look at women as things. The person who is addicted to pornography has no respect for himself, or for anyone else. Substance, relational, or behavioral addictions are really all the same. Sin is sin. However, it does say in First Corinthians 6:18, "Flee from sexual immorality. All other sins a man commits are outside his body, but he who sins sexually sins against his own body" (ESV).

People who treat sex lightly think of others lightly. Pornography is not harmless entertainment. Would you want someone looking at your wife or daughter like that, as an object, a thing without caring emotion or feeling, lusting after them? That woman, that child, is someone's daughter.

> The memories of the sexual sin are a consequence in themselves.

Consequences. We all are responsible for our actions—on earth *and* before God.

Recently a nineteen-year-old mother in our city was charged with child endangerment after she and her newborn baby tested positive for meth. She was charged also with a class D felony offense of interference with custody involving her three-year-old child. She faces up to seven years in prison and loss of her children.

Members of a meth ring were recently sentenced in federal court for conspiring to distribute meth. All sentences are to be served in federal prison without parole.

A fifty-one-year-old woman was sentenced to twenty-one years and ten months.

Her thirty-one-year-old son received fourteen years.

A forty-six-year-old man–ten years.

A forty-two-year-old woman–ten years and one month.

A thirty-five-year-old man–five years and two months.

A thirty-nine-year-old woman–three years and three months.

A thirty-three-year-old man–five years and ten months.

They will live with the consequences of their choices forever.

Those who follow celebrities know many have had problems with addictions. For example, Leif Garrett, a 70's teen idol who is now forty-four, pleaded not guilty to heroine possession in February, 2006, after he was arrested at a Los Angeles subway station. He was once handsome, popular, the idol of teenagers everywhere, had money. But he's spent hard time in prison as the result of his addictions and it shows in his rough and scarred face, and loss of his once thick hair. His demeanor is a bowed head of self-consciousness. The life he once knew is over. After being arrested in February, he checked himself into yet another treatment facility. He's depending on himself, not God, to beat his addictions.

Another example? Jodie Sweetin, former star on the television show Full House, had a crystal meth addiction that landed her in rehab and ruined her marriage. Sweetin was once the perky middle child on the television program. She told *People* magazine in their February 2006 issue, "The drugs were around, I had friends who used them on and off, through high school and college. Then I tried it and it was one of those things where you try it and you think, Well, that was fun, but this won't be a problem for me. It took six months from the first time I tried it to doing it all the time, all day, every day.

Well, that was fun, but this won't be a problem for me.

"When you're on meth you have the most energy in the world. You think, Oh, I could do anything. You're just flying around. You're organizing stupid things, like your sock drawer, over and over again. You have this feeling of total power and ability.

"It becomes this vicious cycle of doing it, feeling horrible afterwards and then just wanting to get high again so you can escape feeling so low.

"There just finally came a point where I thought, I can't do this anymore. It was an accumulation of two years of disappointing myself and disappointing everyone around me. And it was so exhausting." (People Magazine - February 20, 2006)

Jodie Sweetin lost the trust of her husband and her family. She and her husband divorced. After six weeks of inpatient rehab she moved into a house with people from rehab for six months. From a two year addiction to crystal meth, she has been clean eleven months and looks forward to a new life. But it was only by choosing to give up meth and seek help that she has a chance for a new life. She stated in the *People* article, "Life is so good (now)."

Me? I have scars left from the scratching and scabbing. I'm fortunate they're not usually noticeable on my face, arms, chest, legs. I've lost teeth.

Consequences.

When I was first saved I told God, *I've spent seven years of my life in amphetamines, I've racked up bill after bill that I can't pay. All are delinquent. My credit is awful. Now I'm serving You and it's not disappearing. Now I've got to face the consequences of my choices. I don't understand that. I'm Your child. Why wouldn't You remove all that?*

This is where Satan would say, "Let me at her!"

One day a woman came to me and Chris, and cried through the whole conversation, because her children had been taken from her. I was just devastated. I cried out to the Lord for her favor, for her ability to gain custody for her children. As the weeks passed, we continued to meet with her, but she came under the influence of drugs. She kept committing the same sin and ultimately, the consequence was that she did not receive custody of her children again. She wouldn't surrender.

My children should have been taken away from me, while I was under the influence of drugs, but they weren't. A lot of people have had their children taken away. For a long time I walked very gingerly around those people. I didn't want to say that my children hadn't been taken away because I didn't want them to feel they'd done something worse than I did.

I don't understand why my children weren't taken from me, except maybe God had something planned for me that I couldn't do without my family. I repented, meaning I changed my mind, heart, *and* direction.

My consequence, though, was that I had to "get it right" with my kids watching every move I made, mistakes and all. No matter how, why, when, or where, in the end it will glorify God because He knows who can handle the consequences He allows. Whatever the meaning, whatever the consequence of our choices, God knows what He's doing. We have to trust that.

> I had to "get it right" with my kids watching every move
> I made, mistakes and all.

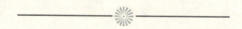

A man we met a couple of years ago works at an in-house facility for teens who struggle with drugs. Before he surrendered his life to Jesus, he was a heroine addict, a needle junkie. He couldn't get through the day without doing large amounts. But now he's totally sold out to the Lord. When he was saved, the desire was taken from him. Not because he said, "Oh God, take the desire from me," and God said, "Beep, the desire's gone my child." It wasn't like that at all. Sometimes God says, "Nope." I'm pretty sure that you're going to go back and do that again unless you have consequences. But sometimes He says, "I believe your heart is true. It's done."

One of the things that Chris has said to the group many times is, "I thought I had done too many bad things to warrant God's forgiveness. I sold drugs to pregnant women; I watched pregnant women put a needle in their arm in front of me with the dope that I had sold them. I thought there was nobody worse than me." Even the consequences of the memories are something we have to surrender to God.

When this man walked into our lives and talked about everything that happened in his life, his testimony really touched my husband.

"I didn't think anyone was ever worse than me," this man said, "or that God could forgive me. But I'm here as a testimony. God is so good. His grace is so big. He loves me just like he loves the person who has walked with Him his whole life; with the same amount of love, the same measure of love."

We know many people who are still walking through a bucket load of consequences; we had to do the same. From finances to having to mend relationships in our family, the understanding God gave us was that we needed to trust Him. He's the one who "started the good work" and He would "see it through to completion."

And we believe Him.

new perspective

I will give them a heart to know that I am the LORD, and
they shall be my people and I will be their God, for they
shall return to me with their whole heart.

Jeremiah 24:7 ESV

I was so blessed to be a part of and to be able to facilitate in
Living Free, our church's recovery ministry, with many different
groups of people. One group called Concerned Persons dealt
with co-dependency. A woman in the first group that I worked
with taught me something important.

At the time I thought I understood that if you did one-
plus-two you're going to come out with three. It was a formula.
Because of what God had done in my life, because He saved
my marriage, because He healed my heart, I looked back and
thought, Well, I did this and this and I trusted the Lord in this,
and I was patient and kind in this so…Suddenly I had a formula
in my head.

I sat down with my co-facilitator and she asked me my
story. We were just getting to know one another so I told her
about my life and how gracious God had been. She was very
quiet, then I asked what her story was.

"Well, I trusted the Lord. I stood on His word, and I believed what He said was true. I cried out to Him for His mercy…" She went down the whole list I'd just given for why God had healed my marriage. Then she said, "And my husband still left me for another woman."

There was no doubt that what she said was one hundred percent from her heart. I could not analyze it and say, Well, she must not have been doing this, or doing that. The Holy Spirit rested right on top of my heart and said, *Now what do you do with your formula?*

> The Holy Spirit rested right on top of my heart and said, *Now what do you do with your formula?*

There is no formula. God is God and His mercy and forgiveness are not logical to most of us. It's not given because we deserve it, but is always what is needed to glorify Him. Each story has individual people who have to make individual choices. God is the Rock we can always hold onto, even when our loved one's choice is to go the other way.

I love the story of Job in the Old Testament. The first time I read it through I thought, *What in the world is this? How horrible! Why would this even be in the Bible?* The second and third time I read it I thought, *Oh, God, you knew this was going to happen! You saw it happening before it happened!*

That is the perfect contrast between God who is *all* and Satan who is a created being. Satan is puffed up, thinking he can one day rule over all. He hates God. Hates His children.

Hates anybody who loves God and serves God. He thought, If I take away everything from Job he's going to say, "I hate you God" because, you see, Satan can't see everything. But God knew His child, Job, and he allowed Satan to test him.

At the end of the story Job's faith was rewarded. Has my own faith been rewarded? Yes, it has. Not always as I thought it would be, but it's definitely been rewarded.

A dear friend gave me something to think about one night when we went to her house for dinner. She came running down the stairs with her Bible and said, "I want to show you what I read today! It's so wonderful!" She flipped to Luke 22:31 where Jesus was talking to Peter and said, *Oh Simon, Simon. Behold Satan has asked to sift you as wheat. But I have prayed for you, Simon, that your faith not fail: And when you have turned back, strengthen your brothers* (NIV). "Jesus already knew that Peter was going to deny Him."

I didn't get the point.

"Oh, that's a neat scripture. I'm glad that spoke to you."

"No, no, no. Listen," she said. "It says, Simon, Simon. Satan has *asked* to sift you as wheat. I knew this but God really spoke to my heart today. Satan can't do anything to us without going to God and asking permission. Because God is in control of our lives."

Then I got it. If we are saved then everything that happens to us is allowed to happen because God is giving us an opportunity to grow in Him, or to fail. It's our choice, but He knows what we're capable of—in Him—knows that we can walk through it. We've got to ask God for the strength because we know the trials are coming because God wants us to grow.

Trials, the hard times, strengthen us. We simply have to realize that and cling to Him. Isn't that wonderful?

While in the drug world, your relationships have been with people you've been up with for weeks on end while doing meth. You've really bared your soul to these people, bared your emotions, your thoughts to these people, and vice versa, so to you, these are the only friends you have. You're afraid that if you turn and walk away from them, what they may think of you. You're afraid of what your husband may do, of what your wife may think, or what your family may do.

Someone walking away from drugs is impressed by someone putting their arms around them saying, you're doing good, you're gonna make it. They rely on their praise to get them through the day. God does give us one another, no doubt, but there has got to be a balance. We learned in Living Free that He gives us three important resources, the Word of God, the Spirit of God, and the people of God. We must be careful that we don't omit the first two resources, or we're just hopping on another merry-go-round.

Why do we care so much about what other people think about us? Sometimes I myself have to go back and read that simple children's story about the Wemmicks to regroup my perspective. We are not a part of this world; we are a part of God's kingdom. We are His ambassadors. Ambassador: a representative of something or someone else. A United States ambassador to another country represents America; he speaks for America. In the same manner we are God's ambassadors to a world that doesn't always acknowledge Him. We cannot be afraid of what that world may think of us. We must have His heart, His mind, His eyes, His understanding.

Even three years after we were saved, Chris and I were still dealing with some changes in our life that weren't comfortable. Different people from church would invite us to their house and we'd think, *Lord help us....We're out of our comfort zone,* which was not necessarily at church, but more with church people. We're not superficial in any way. We're happy, we love being at church. None of that is fake at all. However, to sit down and talk with people—What are your hobbies? How do you feel about this or that issue in life? Small talk was not something we thought we could do, and we were afraid to go through the pain of this learning process.

It was easier in the Tuesday night Living Free open group because we were there with a group of people of like experience but who were not afraid to say exactly what they felt. It's beautiful. We love those people.

The first time Bill and Susann asked us to lunch after church one Sunday we were scared. First of all, they were out of our social league—at least in our mind. Second, we didn't know if we could afford lunch. Third, we were just scared to make friends with normal people who had never experienced or been addicted to the same things that we had. That was *way* outside our comfort zone.

And we were so poor! Chris said, "Do we have enough money in the bank if we have to pay for our own meal?" I was pretty sure we didn't. But we decided we were going to go anyway...maybe call the bank the next day. We had to break free of our fear of socializing with "normal" people.

We drove a 4x4 Jimmy that was rusted along one side and had a crunched front fender. The inside was just…from our life before it was just…yucky. When we started it, this billowing blue-black smoke came from the tailpipe. We also had an old brown car that my husband purchased for 400 dollars. The Jimmy was actually the better of the two so we drove that to church.

Our fears were unrealized. Bill and Susann were wonderful. We had a wonderful conversation with them. They made us comfortable, and they paid for lunch.

God touched that relationship from the very beginning, and every single relationship that He's brought into our lives since. When people come into our life, His hand rests on that relationship if we trust in Him. He blossoms a brand new friendship and it becomes a part of our new "family."

> God touched that relationship from the very beginning, and every single relationship that He's brought into our lives since.

When we began with the Living Free ministry, we worked through a workbook. Part of the exercises was to do a personal audit to see where we stood with God and our family and our church and our friends. The exercise was to make us recognize sins that were keeping us from having solid relationships with each of those groups. We needed to understand that it is sin against God at every single point in our life, whether we're walking away from a lifetime of addiction or whether we've never walked that road, that keeps us from having the kind of relationships we need in our lives.

Ultimately it is us, standing before a holy God. We must ask ourselves, What does He think about where my heart is and what am I doing that's displeasing to God? It's not about earning brownie points with a genie in the sky. It's about what He can give me to make my life better, to glorify Him better.

I have nothing in my heart to give Him, to offer Him, so He's helping me, allowing me to get rid of these sins every day. And I do have to get rid of these sins *daily*. Daily He's filling my heart; He's filling my hands with something that I'm going to be able to glorify Him because I have nothing to give Him on my own. He doesn't do it to puff Himself up. He does it to draw me closer, to have a relationship with me. He *loves* me. It's a perfect relationship.

One Wednesday night Pastor John was talking to us about something that God had laid on his heart that week from Psalm 107, about how we can still cry to the Lord for His mercy, even when the consequence is our own fault. That was brand new to me. I prayed, *Thank you Lord, I needed to hear that. Even though the mess I am in is my fault, I can still call out to You and You will help me.* I began to pray like that. I love learning new things about God. Not that He changes, but that I get to know Him better, to understand His character in all situations is the same. He's merciful. He wants us to ask Him for help.

In our Sunday School class, Bill drew a big circle on the board. He said, "You stand inside the circle and the blessings are right here in the center. That's where we're the farthest away from the edges where danger lies, where all the disappointment is.

But we choose to travel close to the boundary, to the outer edge of the circle, to see how far our thought patterns can go before it's an actual sin. We're to stay well within the boundaries where God's love can reach and bless us. Be careful not to get close to that dangerous outer edge because the farther you are from the center the greater the temptation."

> We're to stay well within the boundaries where God's love can reach and bless us.

Blessings flow to us when we stay in the center of God's love, when we stay right where we're safe. We are drawn within the boundaries of His love when we're forgiven. Why go to the edge where we have to ask Him for forgiveness for the same thing that He forgave us for in the beginning?

When I turned from my sins, the Lord was right there to grab my hand and walk with me. I didn't have to look for Him. He was *there*. Close to me. I felt the warmth of his presence.

A friend told my husband that there was a situation in his life where things came together like the snap of a finger and everything was laid out perfectly. He said he watched it in almost disbelief. He said he turned to look down because he was sure he would see the Savior's feet. He felt the Lord standing right there.

That's how close God is to me all the time. He's right there to take me as soon as I turn from whatever sin is in my life, and to run with me as I experience the victories. Once it was, *Oh, God, I think about meth all the time. I don't know how to control my emotions without it. I don't know how to get through the day without it. I don't know how to clean my house without smoking a joint. You're going to have to help me with this.*

He helped me. I repented. He took away the desire. I did a one-eighty turn and walked away from meth, walked away from pot. I never had any withdrawal symptoms. My God is mighty.

Now, my pills were something else. They were my crutch. For the first year of my salvation I didn't take Mini Thins any more because I had labeled them as "bad." I felt that they were connected with meth and I'd walked away from that. But I started taking MetaboLife. By the hand full. I justified it, telling myself they weren't really a drug. But they were addictive. Every day I woke up and prayed, *Oh God, I pray that you will take this desire away from me. Give me the energy that I need…*

Mind you, I *was* up. I wasn't lying in bed so, obviously, I *had* the energy to get up! I was praying to the Lord to take away the desire while at the same time I was thinking, *Now, how much less today can I take today and still take care of my family and home.* I was still taking pills thinking I couldn't survive without them while praying for God to help me. I said I was trusting God but still swallowing pills. There's little trust, little faith in that.

Thank God for His Holy Spirit who never lets us be comfortable in sin. He soon delivered me from this, too. When I threw them in the trash He took my hand—again. He is ready to take yours too.

living free

Therefore if anyone is in Christ he is a new creation. The old has passed away; behold the new has come.

2 Corinthians 5:17 ESV

Living Free is the name of our church's recovery ministry. There is always an open group format where all who want to come, can come and join in on the topic, and there are closed group formats which lock an assigned group of people together, under specific topics for a certain amount of weeks. I learned that I wasn't alone…that there were others who had issues to deal with and they weren't going to settle for a weekend relationship with God. I was learning how to develop my Christian character, from ground zero.

> …that there were others who had issues to deal with and they weren't going to settle for a weekend relationship with God.

When we first started going to the groups, I thought I would go to "support my husband in his recovery," and found out that God wanted me to be free too. I had watched people for half of my life, in our society, go to counselors, groups, programs, and get "labeled" so they could "understand" themselves better. I didn't want to get to know why I did the things I did, because at the time, I thought that if the fear of going back was going to keep me sober that was all I needed to keep living this new life. However, what I began to learn, through the lessons that were taught, was that God is not a God of fear. Fear should never be the driving force in any recovery. What I learned was contrary to what secular groups teach, "Once an alcoholic/addict always an alcoholic/addict." What God tells us in His word is that when we accept Him as our Lord and Savior, the old is gone, and the new has come; in other words, I am a new person. I had to learn to believe this. To stand on scripture that told me that I had every piece of strength I needed to say no to ungodliness, through God's Spirit living in me. I had to learn how to love with Christ's heart. That meant forgiving everyone that had wronged me, because it wasn't them who was in bondage over the unforgivness, I was. I had to accept that I had worth, and that was a lot harder to accept than the other lessons. When I started applying these things that I learned to my life, God began doing a work in me that took me from fear to rest. I learned that no one wanted to label me in Living Free; they wanted to tell me what God says about whatever issue I was dealing with so that I could deal with it and go on…be free.

Our pastor says, "The Devil knows where your goat's tied, but so does God." When we have God in our lives, the devil can only go as far as his leash extends. He may know where my goat is tied, but God knows that is where Jesus is glorified if I act with the heart and mind of Jesus.

I think about our oldest child's Down Syndrome and all the steps she has to go through just to learn one thing. All of the tiny little steps that have to be programmed into her in just the right way for her to grasp a concept; things that come like a snap of a finger to Samantha. But when that victory comes, it's a celebration. The baby steps we take all come together into a concept known as Christ's character.

> The baby steps we take all come together into a concept known as Christ's character.

One step in the Living Free workbook asked us to write our goals. That was difficult for me. I didn't know how to set goals, how to define them clearly. I see now why it was important to have an objective for each goal. Not just "walk away from this" or "give up this particular thing." Each goal must have a specific aim. For example, My goal is to walk away from meth *in order* to have a better life, to be free, to no longer be afraid.

Another step was to amend my ways then to act on my amends. Amend means to change for the better, to really *make* changes, not just to *want* to make changes. We had to actually go out and reconcile, not to document another person's mistake or to blame others, but to amend our relationships.

Again, in my own life and in seeing other people walk through this, I know that if you take out all the blaming—if *you* hadn't done this—from the conversation and from your thoughts and heart, completely displace it from yourself, then the "amend," or change, actually flows the way God wants. You're then acting on His heart and not your own.

One question was, *Where am I with my church?* That gave me a lot to think about. One of the wonderful things that I see in my church and that I love is that so many people who are active there are ex-addicts or people who have walked away from a lifetime of sin, something they really need to be delivered from. My church says, bring them in. Bring them *all* in. Love them. Let God deal with their hearts. I love that.

Another step had us analyzing our walk with Christ. *I prayerfully continue to walk in the light by unceasingly taking personal inventory of my temptations and sins and by keeping a constant and open relationship with God* (Living Free workbook). God brings to my attention any unforgiveness that I may have harbored. He creates in me a clean heart.

I wasn't asking Him for that. I thought it was just, Oh God, thank You I'm not that way any more. I wouldn't be analyzing my walk with Christ; I wouldn't be asking the Holy Spirit to prompt me. But analyzing my walk means being constantly aware of my relationship with Him. A kind of, How am I doing? Then listening for His answer.

I wrote about where I stood with my husband and my daughters. Later on I had to think about my extended family who had originally been my immediate family—my mother, my brothers, my sister. Where do I stand with them?

I hadn't realized until recently that I needed to forgive my mom, but suddenly tears were flowing. I was very angry at her. Had been for years. When I realized I was angry and had been since I was a child at home, I took it before the Lord. The anger was a foothold for Satan, would be something he could use. I know God brought that to mind because I needed to let go of the anger.

I love my family. They're wonderful people. At Christmas I was able to sit with my siblings one-on-one and tell them how very sorry I was for any holier-than-thou attitude I had. I remember after I was saved, I would pray for the souls of my family…for everyone that didn't know the Lord. I just wanted to go "save the world," go explain to anyone that would listen about this freedom in Christ that I had received. In the process, *my* message was so strong that I chased people off more than it drew them to God. I would have made a great "fire and brimstone" preacher, but that would never help win my family to the Lord. *His* message was, come find peace…come find rest…come find hope.

My husband said it perfectly: "I love your family because you are who you are because of them. You grew up with them." He saw that and I finally see it. Whatever happened in the past, no matter how hard life was growing up, makes no difference now. God is in control of my life now, and how I decide to view all of it, through His eyes is what will determine what happens next.

When Chris and I began to work things out to salvage our marriage, God spoke into our hearts an amazing thing. We'd fought for so long, and even though we were saved, and our marriage was put back together, God was *so good* to be *our Father* and tell us, Shut up, you two. Don't be saying things that tear down one another. Listen to Me.

We understood that everything was going to be taken care of, as long as we listened to God. We had to let God take our hands, our heart, *and our mouths,* and we learned by reading the bible how to treat one another, to stop bringing up the past fights to justify the present fights. Dwelling on it, wallowing in it, wasn't going to help us in our relationship in the *present* or the future.

The Living Free workbook asked us to perform a personal audit. I didn't understand that. What do I do for an audit? I've already got a goal sheet. I've already listed my amends and worked on those. What else do I have to do to identify where I am or where I'm going? But that's exactly what I needed. To identify where I was right then with God, with family, with friends. All my relationships.

Some time later, when Chris and I became facilitators, we put the question on the board, Where do you stand with God? Everybody stared at us. Nobody said a thing. I thought, *Somebody speak.* We could feel their pain as we watched their eyes go from looking at others around them to looking at the floor. The question is something they typically dance around. I remember that feeling. They don't want to answer questions many of them were feeling like, Why are you angry with God?

Where do you stand with God?

Being angry is an acceptable emotion with God. God doesn't punish us for being angry and telling Him about it. Otherwise He would never have given Job what He gave him in the end. Job was angry. He said, "What in the world are you doing to me? I don't deserve this." He was honest with the Lord. It doesn't mean that we can be angry to the point that we're doubting His superiority in our life, but to say, *I'm trying and I'm not seeing any light.* God delights in our honesty.

Another step was to account for my actions. Admitting the exact nature of my wrongs to myself and to others is important. The question then is, Why is it important to admit our wrongs to God? It's easy to go into a counselor's office and admit that we're having issues with a certain thing, struggling with this or that, or we're mad because of this, or we've done this wrong. But to admit it to God?

We *must* because *only* Christ can forgive sin. I have a wonderful friend who has been in therapy all her life because of certain issues. She's told a lifetime of therapists all about everything. She had relied totally on man's wisdom to shed her bad feelings, her anger, her depressions, her disappointments. She's had many therapists say, "Go get a phone book and rip it in two, hit a wall, punch a bag, scream into a pillow. Get out that anger." But the issues were still there. All they taught her how to do was feed the anger.

She's just now learning to tell God about these issues and ask Him for forgiveness. Only God can forgive. Only God can give you closure and peace. Only God can walk you out of whatever situation you're holding on to and into something else and it become an unfolding of a glory-to-glory-to-glory praise.

Another very important step is, *I now ask for forgiveness through Christ and openly acknowledge that I'm forgiven according to scripture* (Living Free Workbook). Accepting God's forgiveness and leaving the sin behind.

Every Sunday and Tuesday I would write on the white board for the open group, Our focus is NOT problem maintenance. Our focus IS transformation through Jesus Christ. That's what happened to Chris and me. We were transformed. Changed. Our mind, our thinking made new.

We didn't start the group with, "Hi. My name is _____ and I'm a _____ addict." Because I'm NOT an addict of anything any more. I don't think about being addicted or about that life. I only recall such things to help others.

I am *made new* and so is Chris. We had to walk through some steps to develop our strength as Christians, and we learned to be *givers* instead of sucking the life out of everyone around us. Our mind, our thoughts, our goals, our focus, are new. They are God's mind. In Him we're made free.

Our mind, our thoughts, our goals, our focus, are new.

Of course, after we're freed from addictions we need to be receivers, in order to heal; receive in order to get back on our feet. Then, one day out of the blue and with much effort in between…ahhh…relief, the strength to help others is just there! Praise God!

blessed obedience

Delight yourself in the Lord and He will give you the desires of your heart.

Psalms 37:4 ESV

A couple of years after I was saved we still had a burden of delinquent debt that we couldn't pay. There was no way we could buy a home, no way to get a good loan for a car. Not without paying the world's price of exorbitantly high interest.

Satan was saying, You can't pay these bills. There's no way. Just get out from under it. If you're serving God with all your heart, shouldn't He be taking care of this?

But God said to me, Hang in there. It's all going to work out. These are the consequences of your choices. I'll give you what you need financially…when I think you can handle it. I'll give you what you need spiritually, every time you ask for it. Come to me for strength…I'll give it to you.

We didn't know how to get past our monthly bills yet we felt that God had told us not to file bankruptcy. He said, Trust in me. That wasn't always easy at first.

Two and a half years ago our church was going through growth and was building a new children's wing. It was the

Because Campaign—because we need more room. Our pastor doesn't like having to ask for money. He said, "The scripture says you should be faithful to your tithe but above and beyond that is called your offering." He said, "Put a seed down. Put a seed down even if it doesn't make any sense."

Chris and I made a pledge. The amount that my husband felt God had laid on his heart was twice what I thought we could do. Actually, the amount he had decided on was the amount that I knew God had laid on my heart but I argued with God. We were sitting in the sanctuary and my "conversation" with God was, *No, there's no way we can pay even half of that so how can we pay all of it? No…No. This can't really be Your voice!* God must find me humorous.

Chris asked, "What can we do? We're supposed to be trusting that God is going to do this. This is God's pledge. Because of it, what God is going to do in us is going to be a miracle. We're going to stand back and say, Thank You for another thing that we can praise You for."

I said, "We have delinquent bills we can't pay down!"

He said, "Honey, you need to pray about this and we need to come to a decision."

It makes no sense that in the middle of our financial problems we were still tithing. But we did it because God said to. He said, See if I don't open up the windows of blessing. You rob Me if you don't give back the tithe. This was over our tithe though, so in my mind, I really thought that if we were still tithing, we were being *obedient enough.* How funny we are to bargain with God on the most ridiculous topic…money…as if He doesn't own everything and can help us with anything.

I really thought that if we were still tithing, we were being *obedient enough.*

When the offering plate came around Chris said, "Write a check for $50."

I said, "We've got $52 in the bank! I've got to put gas in my car; you've got to put gas in your car. It's the beginning of the week and we've got to have groceries and such."

Chris said, "I don't understand it either but I think we just have to trust God."

So I wrote the check with a trembling hand and put it in the offering, not with a happy heart at all but with a fearful heart. I had to ask God to take away that fear.

Obedience. That was hard. But I've learned it's only hard if we are fighting against it.

I don't know how we got through that week. I don't remember how we made it but we didn't borrow and we had gas for the cars, we had food. We gave God the glory for the blessing He gave us.

But after we made the pledge we couldn't make the "payments" because of our financial position. Several months passed. Finally I told Chris that we hadn't been able to make a payment on the pledge. He was so serious when he looked at me and said, "It's not a *payment.* It's not a bill. You *give* to God. Why didn't you come to me earlier?"

I had to ask God to give me joy to write the check, give me courage to write the check.

God was faithful to us because we were obedient to Him. Chris got a promotion at work, a temporary promotion to his boss' position. The company was bought out and through a series of events that seemed like some movie. Chris was promoted permanently.

The promotion meant a better salary for Chris, plus a company vehicle; a nice truck. That meant we didn't have a car payment and didn't have to pay for gas or auto insurance.

All this happened because of our obedience. Because we believed God. It's not reasonable to the world, but it's reasonable to those who belong to Him.

We said to God. *Lord, whatever extra comes in we'll give you half of it back. The other half we're asking that we be allowed to use it to pay off the delinquent bills.*

We were living in this teeny, tiny A-frame house in the middle of a trailer park. We didn't see how in the world we could ever make a house payment more than the $420 a month rent we were paying. We knew people living in two of the trailers dealt meth. We were right in the middle of what we had walked away from and couldn't move away from it because we had tons of debt.

As the extra money began to come in, we gave half of it to the Lord for the Because Campaign and used the other half to begin paying off delinquent debt. Little by little it began to add up until God brought us to the point where we thought we could begin looking for a house. We talked to a friend at church who works for a mortgage company to see what our credit looked like. We knew it had been really junky for a long time so we had no idea what to expect. Our friend said we could get a loan on Chris' credit because we'd gotten that cleaned up, and told us the loan amount we could qualify for.

We began looking at houses in that price range and found we might as well go back to live in the trailer! Our friend told us that if we could pay off a few more things then we could get an FHA loan under both our names. It would stretch us a little financially but we had to do that to get those bills dissolved.

God provided, of course. With the extra checks that came in and a bonus, we paid off that bill and were approved for an FHA loan at a good interest rate. Not the high interest loan that we'd thought we would have to take. God gave us a blessing for being obedient.

But we couldn't find a home that met our needs in the area in which we lived, so we started looking at homes in another town. We'd been looking at homes on a Saturday and our realtor was driving behind us when we passed a yard with a For Sale By Owner sign. Chris said, "Let's stop and look."

I looked at the house. "No way are we going to be able to afford that! That home is too nice for us to live in right now."

But Chris said, "Let's ask."

Our realtor used her cell phone to call the number on the sign. The owner gave her the price which was quite affordable!

We looked at the house after church on Sunday. We walked into that home and it was like the walls were glowing! The carpet was beautiful. The layout of the house was totally original. The craftsmanship was solid. The house only had twelve hundred square feet but it seemed enormous to us as we walked through it. The seller was the builder and he'd lived in it for twelve years.

We loved the house. We walked out onto the red tile patio with a half wall around it.

"Oh my goodness!" I said. "This is so beautiful!"

Chris whispered, "You don't say things like that out loud!" Of course, he was barely keeping his excitement under control.

We went back inside to talk to the owner, trying to be very businesslike, and found the man having a stroke. We went to the neighbor across the street. We paced back and forth in the yard while the neighbor talked to him, praying for the man, thinking, *Oh, Lord, what is going on here? It's not about the house now, it's about this man.*

In the weeks that followed, the owner called the realtor and said he wasn't selling the house because he didn't know what his health might be. So I had to release from myself the desire for that home. I had to pray through this because even that was like a trap from the devil. How are you going to handle this? Are you more concerned about the house…or about this man?

I wanted the house but I prayed and prayed about it. I thought that if that wasn't the home for us and this was a test then I was done with it. I asked God what I was supposed to do in this matter. Am I supposed to say thank you that you've taught me a lesson?

Finally I felt I needed to call this man.

"I'm not going to lie to you. I've been pouting for a few weeks. I want the house because you have a beautiful home. But this has nothing to do with your home. Chris and I were supposed to walk through your house so I could ask you this question. Do you know the Lord Jesus? If you died today would you go to heaven or would you go to hell?"

> If you died today would you go to heaven or would you go to hell?"

The man assured me that if he died he would go to Heaven, and was truly thankful that I would have the heart to ask such a question.

That was the first time I ever asked anybody that question. It was something God wanted me to do.

Chris and I decided we were finished looking at houses. We didn't want to go through that any more right then. But a short time later the home owner called our realtor. He said, "I want to sell to the kids."

Well, by this time we'd blown that house up in our minds to a three thousand square foot home; the floors were marble. So when we walked into the house again everything was just as solid and beautiful as it was before, but it was very tiny. We thought, *Can we live in something this little?* But, we knew it was the right house. The spirit of God had led us right to it, made us see the sign, made us have a conversation with the owner for a reason. It was a blessing from God.

The house appraised for much higher than he was asking! Instant equity. It was a *major* God thing.

We love our home. We planted four trees in our yard this year. We got a dog, as crazy as that may seem in our life right now.

Four years ago I wouldn't have had a goal of being in our own home. I couldn't see past the problems of the day. I knew we couldn't pay the delinquent debt that we had. It was hard to see the blessings were coming. But it happened.

Our pastor reminds us, often, that God wants to be near those who want to be near Him. We want to be near Him.

Yes, God blesses us every day. But the biggest blessing is that He is near to us in a closer relationship. Through Him our desires have changed; changed from what *we* want to what *He* wants of us. He wants us to just love him, and to be obedient.

Am I saying that God blesses us for every stick of obedience? Yes! Do we always see the blessing? No, unfortunately we don't...and yet...fortunately still...we can't always see what God is working out to be the road to bless us. Through this particular experience, God blessed us mostly with the understanding that we needed to ask Him to clean up our hearts some more. We still ask for that today. He is so faithful.

God blessed us mostly with the understanding that we needed to ask Him to clean up our hearts some more.

better than a fairy tale

Rather, speaking the truth in love, we are to grow up in
every way into him who is the head, into Christ.

Ephesians 4:15 ESV

There's an old story someone told me about a man who God
asked to go out and push a big rock in his front yard. The man
said, Lord, I'm going to push that rock out of the way; in Your
name I'm going to move that thing. So he went out and pushed
on the rock...and pushed on the rock. By the end of the day
he was sweaty, thirsty, tired. The next day he said, Lord, I'm
gonna move that rock; I'm gonna move it for You in Your name,
Lord.

As the story goes, he pushed at that rock for many years.
Finally he said, Lord, I don't understand why You asked me to
move this rock. I've pushed it every single day, I've given you all
my strength, and I still haven't moved it. Then God said, I never
told you to *move* it. I just told you to *push* it. Now because of the
muscles you've developed I've got another job for you.

Sometimes we think we're doing what God asked us to do
but we're not making any progress. We don't understand how
what we're doing will affect anybody else but us, so what if we

fail? It's hard for me but if I persevere like God tells me, then in the end I'm going to be able to stand and not fall. God may be having us build spiritual muscle, to grow in order to glorify Him. It's a lesson I have to learn every day, about a lot of things.

> Sometimes we think we're doing what God asked us to
> do but we're not making any progress.

My girls and I shop for groceries on Tuesday at Wal-Mart. I'm frugal so I "price match." I feel that's being a good steward of what God's given us. I sit at my dining room table every week and I write out that one store has, for example, chicken breasts on sale for X amount of dollars per pound; another has a sale price on an item. When I go to Wal-Mart I have it all written down, especially the meat department items. They know me there because I'm always asking, "I'm trying to price match this. It's at this store. What is the selected meat here that's going to be part of this price match?"

I had gotten help this Tuesday with pork chops. The meat man pointed out the ones that were the price match for that particular comp ad. It was a really good deal. I took a couple of packages. I thought, *Thank You Lord for this blessing.*

Usually when I get to the checkout I lay all my stuff on the conveyor belt then put all my price match items separate. The clerk rings up everything and I load it in the cart and by the time they come to the price match section, I take out my list and I'm able to tell them what store, how much per pound, and so forth. I've never had issues with it. Wal-Mart has a big notebook with all the comp ads in it so if they've ever had a question they can go look at it.

Well, the pork chop price match came from an Apple Market and Wal-Mart didn't have that ad. The checker said the Apple Market price was more than half off the Wal-Mart price so they'd need to see the ad. I said I'd never had problems with this before and she could call the store or something but this is what the meat man helped me with.

"Just go ahead and ring everything up and set this aside. You can check it out and I'll pay for it separately."

The clerk tried to check with the meat department but the man who helped me wasn't there. The Customer Service Manager called Apple Market and finally came back to tell me the pork chops I had weren't the cut featured in the Apple Market ad.

"I would never have just run back there and picked it up. I'm a Christian woman and I *don't* lie."

By this time ten minutes had passed and my girls were fidgety. I was terribly embarrassed by this point. Everybody was looking at me. I thought, *I'll just go to Apple Market and get the meat.* The Apple Market wasn't far from my home.

But the CSM returned, and said she had found the gentleman in the meat department that had helped me.

"He said he did help you with this. It's the wrong cut, but we're going to give it to you for that price."

"No," I said, "you're not. If it's not the cut of meat the ad said then that's not right, not fair."

I thought I was going to prove my point.

"No, no—"

I was putting coats on my kids, making sure they were bundled up. I was just going to say, Thank you for your time, then leave the store, flushed cheeks, ears red, burning.

But I looked up and the checker was rolling her eyes. I marched right back to her.

"I'm not going to take the meat," then I basically ripped her apart with my tongue. "You should not have rolled your eyes at me. That was rude."

"I'm sorry."

"You should be."

I thought, *You are not going to treat me like that,* huff-huff-huff.

We were on our way to the car when Samantha, my soon-to-be seven-year-old said, her eyes big, "Mom, I've never seen you act like that before, never heard you say things like that before."

That was a God thing in itself.

By the time we got to the car I'd said things like, "Even Jesus got mad when they were selling things in the temple and he threw the tables over." The more I was talking the more I was feeling like the biggest hypocrite on the face of the earth.

I realized I was creating lies to make myself feel better. Just like when I was a child, when I needed to make myself look better to someone. Even telling this I feel like, "yuk," small inside. That's how I felt then. Small and so stupid that I could let the enemy (Satan) again have my tongue, my emotions. I know I'm human, and I *know* that I'm no angel. I'm not perfect but I need to stand up and say, "I'm a child of the living God; I'm not going to act that way." I had thrown God's name up to that young woman and then cut her apart with what was supposed to be God's tongue.

I had thrown God's name up to that young woman and then cut her apart with what was supposed to be God's tongue.

When I'd loaded everything into the car I said, "Samantha, we're going back inside."

She said, "Why?"

I said, "I need to apologize to that young lady."

She said, "But mom, she was wrong."

I said, "You know what? It doesn't matter. I don't know how terribly wrong she was really, but it doesn't matter."

Then I explained to her that sometimes humility means just bucking up and taking the blame even if it's not yours. Then I was able to tell her that Jesus died on the cross and He took all my blame. A sinless, perfect God came from a perfect heaven to a junky world, a world he created to be wonderful and we junked up. He was separated from the Father for a time so He could take all my sin, all this yucky stuff, to the grave. Because of that, whether I was right or wrong, I was going to apologize for cutting that woman up with my tongue.

I went back into the store and as the Customer Service Manager came toward me, I started bawling like a baby. I was just a big bundle of emotions, so embarrassed. I told her I needed to talk to the checker and apologize. She said everything was all right but I insisted. I told the checker, "I'm sorry I was so mean."

She said, "I'm sorry, too. I wasn't rolling my eyes at you. It was at the meat department man. They do this all the time—"

I said, "It doesn't matter if you were or were not doing it at me. I still am so sorry and I'm asking you to forgive me." She was just shocked that I would ask her to forgive me.

There was where Jesus was glorified. Not in me standing up for my rights. But in humbling myself and asking forgiveness.

Now I carry all my ads with me in a little zip lock bag along with my list. Now it's all *really* organized. I went to Wal-Mart the other day and when the same Customer Service Manager came walking up to help me I thought, *Oh, no-no-no.* But I had to kind of chuckle and she did, too. In that moment God was glorified again and I grew a little stronger.

My life is so different than it was just a few years ago. It's better than a fairy tale. When I was a kid I had the dreams all little girls have of being a princess, marrying a prince, living in a castle. My life is better than a dream because I didn't know then that the real fairy tale life is in living with God.

When we began working with the Living Free program as facilitators, I loved seeing Chris take charge. I don't know what kind of woman I'd have been without him. I don't know what kind of mom I would have been without him. I would have tried very hard to be a godly mom and to walk out my faith like God wanted me to, but there are times when I don't make good decisions. I'll say something to the children and immediately my husband will pull me aside.

"I don't know how wise that was."

It makes me stop. *I think I was just trying to be boss right then instead of trying to teach my children how to be responsible adults. I think I was just trying to say, "Because I said."*

> *I think I was just trying to be boss right then instead of trying to teach my children how to be responsible adults.*

That balance, that wisdom, wasn't there for a long time. I'm not saying Chris was a bad father. He just…wasn't there. Now I don't know what I'd do without him.

The other day I lost my keys. All I had was a car key. That evening I was out and when I got home, and I found the door locked. I rang the doorbell. Chris came to the door and opened it just a little.

"You gotta go around," then he shut the door in my face.

I thought, *Huh?* I went to the other door that led into the kitchen. He'd unloaded the dishwasher but there were dishes from ice cream and all kinds of stuff in the sink and I thought, *Huh!* Then I walked around the corner and found that in the living room Chris and the girls had built a tent. They'd used all the sheets and blankets from the linen closet and all the chairs and they'd built this great big tent.

I said, "Hello?"

They jumped up, "Yaaah!" and started hitting me with pillows!

"You almost blew it," Chris said. "It was supposed to be a surprise."

Years ago when I dreamed of a family, this was what I dreamed. Thank You, God.

When Chris and I went Christmas shopping this year, I found some jeans that I thought were so cute. Little corduroys. I thought, *Samantha is going to love these.* Well, Chris, my sensible husband, disagreed.

"She's not going to like the way they fit. She's going to like these."

He held up a little pair of basic jeans. They had a few little funky pockets on them but they were basic blue jeans.

"You want to make a bet?" I was thinking, *She's gonna like the pizzazz, not the plain.*

When she put them on Samantha said she liked the ones her dad got her better. I was disappointed.

"I thought you'd like these."

I really wanted her to like the jeans that I got her.

"You know, mom…"

She always makes sure there is no offense when she says something but she's also to the point.

"No offense, mom, but dad would know the kind of jeans that I like because we spend the most time together."

At first that was like a big dagger in my heart. I thought, *What do you mean? I work fewer hours than he does, we come home and read Narnia, we spend time together. She gets up with me in the morning and we read the Bible together,* but I swallowed my hurt feelings. You see, to a child, having special times with their father is amplified into fairy tales in their hearts, that they will replay over and over…making it seem like "the most time." So awesome!

"You and dad have been spending a lot of time together. That's wonderful, isn't it?"

When I said that out loud it released all the jealousy in me. I thought, *Praise God that my daughter thinks, "My daddy spends tons of time with me."* When she grows up she will look for a man who will set aside time to be with her, who she sees roll over in the morning and grab the Bible and start reading where he left off the previous morning. That's the kind of man I pray she looks for. A man like her daddy.

That's the kind of man I pray she looks for.

But if Chris and I had kept going down the path of drug addiction she would have been looking for a man she felt she could fix, because that was the kind of life I was living. I praise God that He gave all of us this second chance. Isn't that great? Isn't God great!

my hope-your hope

> But grow in the grace and knowledge of our Lord and
> Savior Jesus Christ. To him be the glory both now and to
> the day of eternity. Amen.
>
> II Peter 3:18

A family of four were sitting at the dinner table when the teenage daughter asked, "Dad, mom, can we go to the movies tomorrow?"

The mother replied, "Sure honey, what are you going to see?"

The girl began to explain which movie they were going to see and by the end of the conversation, had to confess that it was an R rated movie. They also argued that all of their friends from church had seen it, and it only had a *little* bit of bad stuff in it, so "what was the big deal?" After a lengthy debate on the importance of "guarding your minds" from the mom and the dad, the father explained that it was time that the kids were old enough to make their own choices…and that the kids knew right from wrong and left it at that.

The next day, the teenage group came rushing into the house to tell the dad how great the movie was and that it really was just a *small* amount of bad language and other stuff so it was okay. As they came into the kitchen, the smell of their father's famous homemade brownies filled the air. "Wow, just in time, thanks dad!" and they began to eat. But before they could put the brownies into their mouths, the father wanted to let them know that there was just one thing that they needed to hear.

"Now these are indeed my famous brownies, but today, I have put just a *little* bit of dog poop into the batter. Now, it shouldn't matter, because it was just a *small* amount and so it's okay."

When I heard this story, it was a turning point for me. I knew that it was a silly story that was told to help us understand that we should guard our spirits...that even a little bit of bad is still bad. My husband and I knew that we needed to get rid of a lot of things that we tolerated, because the Holy Spirit had been telling us to do just that. God used this silly joke to drive home in our hearts that to tolerate the sitcoms that we were used to watching, and to even have the R rated movies that were still in our house, was too much tolerance. We had been set apart by a holy and merciful God and we were acting like spoiled children and saying to Him, "What's the big deal?"

> We had been set apart by a holy and merciful God and we were acting like spoiled children and saying to Him, "What's the big deal?"

I'm not talking about legalism, where someone thinks that they have to do everything just right to win God's approval; I'm talking about obedience. It was about the same time that we met a woman that worked at Teen Challenge, and she challenged us to read Ephesians 5:1–20 for a month and to see what we thought in the end. We took the challenge and came to the end of the month with a new attitude about our walk with Christ. You see, we all need to come to the place where we see God for who He is. He knows what is the very best for us, because He made us! If we trust Him for the very best, we will obey what He tells us to do.

I have tried to place, throughout the book, places of rest and places to help someone connect and fill up on God's treasures, but it all boils down to the renewing of the mind. My mind doesn't think the way it used to think. I don't act out of selfish ambition and self centered motives. I invited the Spirit of God to come and purge me of all the things that are useless and hurtful. He is faithful. He is still working on me, and will be till the end of my time here on earth. When we give God the steering wheel, He will take us to places of safety, and places where we can renew our strength. This is not possible for those who have not given their lives to Christ. Inviting Him in is only the beginning. We were given new hearts on the day we surrendered, but He told us to retrain our actions based on His word. The Holy Spirit helps us by telling us to stop listening to stuff on the radio if it takes our minds back to thoughts of our former life. We listened to Him and got rid of all the secular music that we listened to before our salvation. It took our minds back to remembering the things of "before."

First John has become one of my favorite books from God's Word. It talks about walking out your faith, being accountable, and even having accountability with other people. God's word tells me that it is good to have accountability with one another, but you can't rely on that to be your closure because *only* God can forgive sin. Only God can give you rest and peace and walk you out of an addiction and into a new life of freedom. I had to realize that I could talk to a lot of people about a lot of things, but it was ultimately God who was going to tell me the truth about what would be best for me.

It was God's Word that came alive and became my personal instruction booklet for life. The passage from Ephesians from earlier is the one that helped me put God's character in perspective. He wants us to be safe and happy and whole, and He tells us how we can do that. I chose to believe Him and He was, as always, faithful to give me all I needed. A verse in First John tells us God is light. Not even a shadow of darkness exists in Him. The meth world is a dark world. When I stepped out of the drug world, out of that darkness, God met me. He was waiting for me. When you are in the dark and someone in the lead has a flashlight, *they* know where the rocks and the twigs are because they have the light. You're stumbling around behind them. The only way *you* feel secure and you're not stumbling over everything, is if you have the light. You know where you're pointing it; it's shedding light on the path. That is who God is in my life. God is my light. I'm no longer in the dark. I'm not following anybody else. I can't. It's not just about being accountable to another person. It's about being accountable to God, about letting Him be my light and letting that bless the relationship that I have with everyone else.

It's about being accountable to God

Our pastor tells us often that God didn't intend for us to be Lone Ranger Christians. That doesn't mean we come and dump all our "stuff" in the middle of a group of people all the time, but it does mean that God appoints certain people to be a part of our lives. Accountability to a "group" is not bad, but if that's the only thing that's keeping you on your path, you are not experiencing freedom. Many people I have met through the years who have gained their freedom from drugs or alcohol through AA or NA are still attending the groups sometimes as often as three times a week. They know the times and dates of the groups in other towns as well, just in case they are there. They feel that they have to go to the groups to remain free; to have accountability to be able to say "no" to whatever substance they have walked away from. I can honestly say that I am free. I don't go to the groups to remain free. I go to the groups to meet other people that need to hear the message of freedom. God is ready to take upon Himself, all of the issues that cause the addiction in the first place. No band aid. Total healing.

My life now represents joy and peace, hope and a future. The chains are gone, and I am standing outside of the prison to tell those who are in bondage, that there is hope and a future for them too! I am sure of it. I am not afraid that I might be wrong about this, because I know it to be true. It is what God tells us in His Word, and I am living proof of it.

> I am standing outside of the prison to tell those who are in bondage, that there is hope and a future for them too!

My new addiction, I guess you would have to say, is God. Only, this dependence doesn't leave me depleted and full of remorse. I know that I am not running from issues or people or even myself anymore. I love to pray, to lay it all down to my Father, who hears all of my words and lets me talk honestly about everything.

We have a friend who when she sees us asks, "How's your devotion been? What has God been speaking to you lately?" That's a hard one for me because I can talk, and talk, and talk. It's hard for me to be still, to just listen. However, when I'm quiet is when I can hear the voice of my Savior talking to me. His voice tells me the truth about everything, and tells me that I do have the courage to stand with strength. She holds me accountable to the "listening end" of my devotion time with God. Having these kind of friends is what I have longed for all of my life. We have opened ourselves up, and allowed ourselves to be vulnerable, and what we got in return is wonderful Kingdom friends. Even this is a renewing of the mind. When we were afraid, we had to listen to God tell us the truth. That when we trusted Him, He would help us and even sometimes move mountains to connect us to the right people. We have to choose to believe Him.

The way we talk has to change. If we are going to say that we belong to the Creator of the universe, and that He calls us His children, then we better be prepared to have the things that come out of our mouths to be good things. Sometimes we have to tell ourselves the truth, according to what God's word says. If God says that I can do all things through Christ, then I will choose to believe it and say it out loud. At first it isn't easy to say "I have been delivered. I'm not going back. I've repented." But the more you say it out loud the more your heart believes it's attainable. It's not like a chant—this is what I am, this is what I am, this is what I am. But the more you speak the truth out loud the more it becomes a part of you. Your first language. We must stand on the scripture that says—He who is set free is free indeed. When we're set free in Christ we are a new creature. We're not the person we once were. Period.

When we come to Christ, surrender to the Lord Jesus, we must surrender *everything* to Him. How do we do that? It's easier than you think. The thinking about it is way harder than the "doing." I used up a lot of years worrying about giving up my freedom to make my own choices. I was afraid of God's wisdom, because I thought it was all about rules. All about what I would have to do, and what I could not do. I was very wrong.

The thinking about it is way harder than the "doing."

God tells us how to live because He wants the very, very best for us. It is a matter of trust to do what He says. The first thing that He tells us is that we have to surrender to Him. Make Him Lord, or ruler of our thoughts, words and actions. We have to come to the point of asking Him to be in charge. Remember, He wants the very best, so it's about making a choice to have fullness in this life and have eternal life with Him. When I gave my heart to Jesus, I recognized that the Lord was real and beautiful and compassionate and strong and merciful and bigger than me. I knew that He left Heaven and came here for me. Put skin on for me. Died for me. Because He loves me that much. This realization made me so grateful that I knew beyond the shadow of any doubt that I wanted to be with Him forever. I wanted to trust Him with my life. And that I needed Him to forgive me. That is why I am obedient to Him, because I love Him. All the fear disappeared in regards to losing my freedom because what I gained was freedom. Free to live the very best.

Even the steps that I have taken in my life since I have given my heart to the Lord have been worth all of the energy and effort in dealing through the pain that lay underneath. When I finally started seeing things through Jesus' eyes, I began to almost laugh at the things that kept me paralyzed for so long. I don't mean to discount the pain that comes with painful situations, but in the same sense I was no longer bound to the circumstances. The things that I witnessed as a child no longer made me angry; I began to have Jesus' heart concerning my father. I grieve for my father's soul. I am not sure that he made a commitment to the Lord, I can only hope.

About six months before my father's death, he began calling me and we began to talk about God. He asked if I was really a Christian, and I was so excited to tell him about my relationship with Christ. Sometimes he would call me when he was drunk and tell me that God was working on him and he was going to make the right choice soon. I would leave those conversations crying, and wondering if I was ever going to get through to him. Soon, I got a phone call from my dad's girlfriend telling me that he was in the hospital. Through the next few weeks, he had a couple of surgeries and he finally slipped into a semi-coma and was unable to talk anymore. I went to my father's side and shared with him one last time the message of forgiveness and told him that all he had to do was think it, if he could not say it. He had tears in his eyes when I told him these things. He died soon after that.

I would never have been able to do this with my father if I was still bound to the unforgiveness that plagued my life for so long. I was able to walk through the pain of suffering the loss yet again of losing my father. At first forgiving my father, or even my mother, was a choice, because I knew that God said that it was the best for me, to trust Him. In the end, I have a great relationship with my mom, and God has given me differ-ent eyes to see her with. I understand that she would have loved to be free from all of the stuff that piled onto and into her life. Things that paralyzed her and made her feel worthless. I hate that that happened to my mom, but she knows the way out now. That is God's heart, that we all understand that.

He'll be there for you just like He was there for me the day I fell on my knees in that little trailer and poured out my sin. You have to ask honestly, open everything to Him, *and make Him Lord of everything in your life.* He is faithful.

> open everything to Him, *and make Him Lord of every-thing in your life.*

I trust that God is right there in my dining room every single morning when I pray to Him, when I read His word, when I ask Him for guidance. I believe He's sitting right next to me, standing right next to me. He's holding me some morn-ings, mornings that I have a grief in my heart. Some mornings He rejoices with me, shares my joy at just spending time with Him.

This is my story—so far. I was addicted to meth for seven years, to pot, pills and alcohol for almost half my life. My husband and I both were lost in that trap. I felt no hope.

But this is the story of deliverance.

Once I gave my heart to the Lord, I was no longer slave to that old master. I serve a new master—the Lord Jesus. I am no longer bound by drugs and alcohol, or even people or things. God gave me a new heart and a new mind—a mind over meth—to think with, to experience Him with.

Thank you God. I am free! I am free! I am free!

This is not the end.

definitions

Habit

Custom; regular way of doing

Addict

Person who cannot stop doing something which is harmful.

Addiction

Inability to stop taking a drug. When we think of addiction we usually think of alcohol or drug addictions but there are many types of addictions. A workaholic has an addiction. So does the man who fills his yard with cars. Watching eight hours of television a day is an addiction, just like having to continuously clean your home or your hands are an addiction.

Methamphetamine

A derivative of amphetamine, a powerful stimulant that affects the central nervous system. Amphetamines were originally intended for use in nasal decongestants and bronchial inhalers and have limited medical applications, which include the treatment of narcolepsy, weight control, and attention deficit disorder. Meth can be smoked, snorted, orally ingested, and injected. It is accessible in many different forms and may be identified by color, which ranges from white to yellow to darker colors such as red and brown. Meth comes in a powder form that resembles granulated crystals and in a rock form known as "ice," which is the smokeable version of meth that came into use during the 1980s.

Meth modifies the brain's pleasure receptors by producing excess levels of dopamine, a natural chemical found in the brain. The excess dopamine produced by meth usually allows users to experience a fairly rapid but brief rush, followed by a longer period of euphoria. Following the period of euphoric sensation is the crash—a longer period of lethargy, depression, paranoia, and even violent or aggressive behavior. With prolonged use, a meth user's ability to experience normal levels of pleasure declines and is replaced by extreme boredom with normal day-to-day activities. It is this scenario that makes meth a highly addictive drug that creates powerful cravings in the user.

Side effects of use include convulsions, dangerously high body temperature, stroke, cardiac arrhythmia, stomach cramps, and shaking. Some abusers, while refraining from eating and sleeping, will binge on meth. During these binges, users will inject as much as a gram of meth every two to three hours over several days until they run out of the drug or are too dazed to continue use.

Chronic meth use can lead to psychotic behavior including intense paranoia, visual and auditory hallucinations, and out-of-control rages that can result in violent episodes. Chronic users at times develop sores on their bodies from scratching at "crank bugs," which describes the common delusion that bugs are crawling under the skin. Long-term use of meth may result in anxiety, insomnia, and addiction.

Chronic meth abuse can result in inflammation of the heart lining and, for injecting drug users, damaged blood vessels and skin abscesses. Social and occupational connections progressively deteriorate for chronic meth users. Acute lead poisoning is another potential risk for meth abusers because of a common method of production that uses lead acetate as a reagent.

Medical consequences of meth use can include cardiovascular problems such as rapid heart rate, irregular heartbeat, increased blood pressure, and stroke-producing damage to small blood vessels in the brain. Hyperthermia and convulsions can occur when a user overdoses and, if not treated immediately, can result in death. Research has shown that as much as fifty percent of the dopamine-producing cells in the brain can be damaged by prolonged exposure to relatively low levels of meth and that serotonin-containing nerve cells may be damaged even more extensively.

Long-term meth use can cause permanent and severe physical and psychological problems, including severe weight loss, rotting teeth, scars and open sores, a variety of cardiovascular problems, convulsions, and hallucinations. Meth-induced paranoia can result in homicidal and suicidal thoughts. Using brain imaging techniques, scientists have found that damage done to the dopamine neurons by long-term meth use remained for as long as three years after meth use was stopped. Research is continuing.

You don't have to be a meth user to be affected by meth. The manufacture of meth presents a substantial risk of injury and even death to those who live in or near drub labs. Chemicals found in these labs can enter the body through inhalation of gasses produced by the manufacturing process. The acidic gasses released in meth production can immediately cause second or third degree burns of the skin, and extreme pain and even death if inhaled. Meth lab chemicals can be absorbed through contact with the skin, a danger that occurs both from cooking meth and from storing chemical ingredients.

The effects of taking these toxic materials into the body through inhalation or absorption may be temporary or permanent, immediate or delayed, mild or severe, and can injure the lungs and skin, the liver and kidneys, and the nervous system. Eating contaminated foods and beverages, or placing contaminated objects such as containers or toys in the mouth leads to ingestion of these dangerous chemicals. Ingestion of some of the chemicals used to make meth can cause psychosis, seizures, and, in high doses, death.

Young children, because they crawl and play on the floor and put their hands and other objects into their mouths, are at a much greater risk than are adults for ingestion and absorption of these chemicals. Children's different metabolic processes, including more rapid respiration and higher metabolic and growth rates, also place them at an increased risk of chemical exposure from inhaled, absorbed and ingested toxins.

Meth abuse during pregnancy can cause prenatal complications such as increased rates of premature delivery and altered neonatal behavior patterns, such as abnormal reflexes and extreme irritability, and may be linked to congenital deformities. Meth abuse, particularly by those who inject the drug and share needles, can increase users' risks of contracting HIV/AIDS and hepatitis B and C.

There are no pharmacological treatments for meth dependence. Antidepressant medications can be used to combat the depressive symptoms of withdrawal. The most effective treatment for meth addiction is cognitive behavioral interventions, which modify a patient's thinking, expectancies, and behavior while increasing coping skills to deal with life stressors.

Psychology Today:
October 10, 2002

According to a survey released by the National Association of Counties documented in USA Today on January 18, 2006, methamphetamine accounts for more emergency room visits than any other drug.

The survey of 200 hospitals run or funded by counties in 39 states and Washington D.C., shows that 47% said meth is the top illicit drug involved in emergency room visits. Sixteen percent said pot, and 15% said cocaine. "This is a national problem," association spokesman Tom Goodman said. "The costs of meth are placing a great strain on county governments."

Nearly 12 million people in the U.S. have used meth at least once in their lives, according to responses to the 2004 National Survey on Drug use and Health conducted by the Department of Health and Human Services. About 1.4 million had used meth in the past year.

Bill Hansell, president of the National Association of Counties and a county commissioner in Umatilla County, Oregon, said meth abuse can damage an entire community. Local governments pay to clean up toxic waste left by home meth labs, to care for the neglected children of addicts, and to provide treatment.

USA TODAY

January 18, 2006

According to The National Household Survey on Drug Abuse conducted by the Substance Abuse and Mental Health Services Administration in 2001, an estimated 16.6 million Americans (7.3% of the population) abuse drugs and alcohol. Also, 22 million people abuse alcohol only, while 5.6 million people abuse illicit drugs. In addition, the survey found that 4.6 million drug abusers do not believe they have a problem.

Psychology Today

September 17, 2002

Cocaine

Cocaine is a powerfully addictive stimulant that directly affects the brain. Cocaine is a Schedule II drug, meaning that it has high potential for abuse. Cocaine is generally sold on the street as a fine, white, crystalline powder known as coke, C, snow, flake, or blow. Cocaine is a stimulant that makes users feel high, euphoric, energetic, and mentally alert after taking the drug. It is a highly addictive drug that can cause severe mental and physical problems; cocaine overdose can cause death. Once having tried cocaine, an individual cannot predict or control the extent to which he or she will continue to use the drug.

Cocaine is a strong central nervous system stimulant that interferes with the reabsorption process of dopamine, a chemical messenger associated with pleasure and movement. It gives its user a false sense of limitless power and energy. When users "come down," they are usually depressed, edgy, and craving for more. An appreciable tolerance to the high may be developed, and many addicts report that they seek but fail to achieve as much pleasure as they did from their first exposure. In rare instances, sudden death can occur on the first use of cocaine or unexpectedly thereafter. There is no way to determine who is prone to sudden death.

Long term effects include:
Dependence

Depression

Feelings of restlessness, irritability, mood swings, paranoia, sleeplessness, and weight loss. Emotional problems and isolation from family and friends

Psychosis, paranoia, depression, anxiety disorders, and delusions

Damage and holes on the inside of the nose and inflamed nasal passages

Increased risk of hepatitis and HIV

Severe respiratory infections

Heart attacks, chest pain, respiratory failure, strokes, and abdominal pain and nausea

Warning signs of cocaine use:
Red, bloodshot eyes

A runny nose or frequently sniffing

A change in eating or sleeping patterns

A change in groups of friends

A change in behavior

Acting withdrawn, depressed, tired, or careless about personal appearance

Losing interest in school, family, or activities previously enjoyed

Frequently needing money

Psychology Today

October 10, 2002

Alcohol

Nearly 14 million people in the United States–1 in every 13 adults–abuse alcohol or are alcoholic. Alcohol problems are highest among young adults ages 18–29. People who start drinking at an early age–for example, at age 14 or younger–greatly increase the chance that they will develop alcohol problems at some point in their lives.

Alcohol abuse differs from alcoholism in that it does not include an extremely strong craving for alcohol, loss of control over drinking, or physical dependency. Alcohol abuse is defined as a pattern of drinking that results in one or more of the following situations within a 12-month period:

Failure to fulfill major work, school, or home responsibilities

Drinking in situations that are physically dangerous, such as wile driving a car or operating machinery

Having recurring alcohol-related legal problems, such as being arrested for driving under the influence of alcohol or for physically hurting someone while drunk

Continued drinking despite having ongoing relationship problems that are caused or worsened by the drinking

Symptoms of alcoholism or alcohol dependence:

Craving: a strong need, or compulsion, to drink

Loss of control: the inability to limit one's drinking on any given occasion

Physical dependence: withdrawal symptoms such as nausea, sweating, shakiness and

Anxiety occur when alcohol use is stopped after a period of heavy drinking

Tolerance: the need to drink greater amounts of alcohol in order to "get high"

Solitary drinking

Secretive about drinking behavior

Symptoms of alcohol abuse:

People who abuse alcohol can identify if they have a drinking problem if they have:

Considered reducing the amount of alcohol consumed

Become annoyed by criticism of drinking behavior

Experienced guilt feeling about drinking behavior

A drink first thing in the morning (as an eye opener) in order to get rid of a

Hangover or to steady their nerves

Yes to one or more of these suggests a possible alcohol problem.

Health hazards:

    Increased incidence of cancer, particularly cancer of the lar-
ynx, esophagus,

    liver and colon

    Acute and/or chronic pancreatitis

    Cirrhosis of the liver

    Alcoholic neuropathy

    Alcoholic cardiomyopathy

    High blood pressure

    Nutritional deficiencies

    High blood pressure

    Erectile dysfunction

    Cessation of menses

    Fetal alcohol syndrome in the children of women who drink
during pregnancy

    Depression

    Traffic fatalities

    Accidental deaths

    Increased risk of suicide

    Wernicke-Korsakoff syndrome

Psychology Today

October 10, 2002

Marijuana

Pot is a green or gray mixture of dried, shredded flowers and leaves of the hemp plant Cannabis sativa. It is the most often used illegal drug in this country. There are over 200 slang terms for pot, including pot, herb, weed, boom, Mary Jane, gangster, and chronic.

Within a few minutes of inhaling pot smoke the user will likely feel, along with intoxication, a dry mouth, rapid heartbeat, some loss of coordination and poor sense of balance, and slower reaction time. The users eyes look red. A user who has taken a very high dose of the drug can have severe psychotic symptoms and need emergency medical treatment.

Pot hinders short-term memory (memory for recent events). The user may have trouble handling complex tasks. Use affects many skills required for safe driving: alertness, the ability to concentrate, coordination, and reaction time, make it difficult to judge distances and react to signals and sounds on the road. When users combine pot with alcohol, as they often do, the hazards of driving can be more severe than with either drug alone.

Someone high on pot may:

Seem dizzy and have trouble walking

Seems silly and giggly for no reason

Have very red, bloodshot eyes

Have a hard time remembering things that just happened

When the early effects fade, over a few hours, the user can become very sleepy

It's common for pot users to become engrossed with ordinary sights, sounds, or tastes, and trivial events may seem extremely interesting or funny. Time seems to pass very slowly, so minutes feel like hours. Sometimes the drug causes users to feel thirsty and very hungry—an effect called "the munchies."

Parents should look for these signs in their children's behavior, though it may be difficult with teenagers. However, these signs may also indicate problems other than use of drugs.

Withdrawal

Anxiety

Distorted perception

Loss of coordination

Panic attacks

Daily cough and phlegm

Symptoms of chronic bronchitis

More frequent chest colds

Depression

Fatigue

Carelessness with grooming

Hostility

Deteriorating relationships with family members and friends

Changes in academic performance

Increased absenteeism or truancy

Loss of interest in sports or other favorite activities

Changes in eating or sleeping habits

Parents should also be aware of:

Signs of drugs and drug paraphernalia, including pipes and rolling papers

Odor on clothes and in the bedroom

Use of incense and other deodorizers

Use of eye drops

Clothing, posters, jewelry, etc., promoting drug use

Network of friends who use drugs and urge them to do the same

Researchers have found that children and teens (both male and female) who are physically and sexually abused are at greater risk than other young people of using pot and other drugs and of beginning drug use at an early age.

Psychology Today
October 10, 2002

Scripture Support

Forgiveness

Acts 26:17–18

1 John 2:2

Ephesians 1:7

Born Again

John 3:3–7

John 3:16

2 Corinthians 5:17–21

Romans 6:9–11

Philippians 2:12–13

1 John 1:7

Abiding in God
    2 Corinthians 3:18
    John 14:13
    John 15:4
    Matthew 11:28

Assurance
    Hebrews 13:5
    John 11:40
    Romans 5:10
    1 John 2:2

Prayer
    Luke 11
    1 Thes. 5:17
    Matthew 6:6
    Matthew 7:9
    John 14:12

Oneness with God
    Romans 6:4
    John 10:3
    Galatians 2:20

Obedience
    John 14:15
    1 Thes. 5:17
    John 15:4
    Luke 14:26–27, 33
    Matthew 7:13–14
    Joshua 24:15

Temptation/Trouble
John 16:33
1 Corinthians 10:13
Hebrews 4:15
2 Corinthians 6:4
Romans 8:37
2 Corinthians 5:7
Romans 8:35
John 16:33
John 11:40
Revelations 2:7

Belief
Galatians 5:1
Matthew 6:26–28
2 Corinthians 4:2
Matthew 16:24